Moving to the Country

Moving to the Country

*How to Buy or Build the Place
You've Always Wanted*

Don Skillman

STACKPOLE
BOOKS

Published by
STACKPOLE BOOKS
5067 Ritter Road
Mechanicsburg, PA 17055

Printed in the United States of America

10 9 8 7 6 5 4 3 2 1

First edition

Cover design by Kathleen Peters

Library of Congress Cataloging-in-Publication Data

Skillman, Don.
    Moving to the country: how to buy or build the place you've always
wanted / Don Skillman.
        p.   cm.
    ISBN 0-8117-2445-X (pb)
    1. House buying. 2. Country homes. 3. Real property—Purchas-
ing. 4. Country life. I. Title.
HD1379.S55   1996
333. 33'8—dc20   95-19874
                                                          CIP

Contents

Introduction

The causes vary, but the dream does not. Thousands, no millions, of individuals and families either have moved to the country or are actively planning to do so. The tension of city life in dense, populous mazes, a lifestyle many refer to as the rat race, eventually takes its toll. Doubts about schools persist. Burnout and frustration so dull the enjoyment of life that many who long for a simpler, more peaceful existence become determined to get out. Out to the country, back to nature.

The country! What is this panacea that permeates the dreams and thoughts of so many? It is more than a land where trees grow without concrete rings, where birds sing in the morning, and where streams flow and lakes snuggle in hollows. It is a place where children ride to school in yellow buses that ply country roads and blue highways. Where nearby towns are small, and you know the name of the manager of each of the two local banks. Where there are new shopping malls on the outskirts, but if you want a piece of black stovepipe or some heat tape you go to the old hardware store downtown.

For country dwellers, a trip to the city can be anything from a few dozen to hundreds of miles. And in the city, you again find rush-hour traffic, ghettos, high rises, dirt, filth, crime, pressure, hurry, tension, and all the other plagues that humans inflict on themselves and each other. The negatives you left behind are all there to provide comparisons with the slower pace at which you now live. You can visit the city and come away feeling smug; more than smug, really, you feel extremely fortunate.

Country folks are not faced with commuting to work in heavy traffic. What traffic there is will usually be friendly, and often a good portion is made up of people you know. You will soon come to know your neighbors, your children's teachers, the local merchants and storekeepers, and those who provide various services.

It is a friendly place, this country world, and it's no wonder that so many people long to become a part of it. And the country provides a good environment in which to raise young people.

The air is cleaner, so clear you can see the stars at night. You know when the seasons change by the green grass of spring, the summer sun, the kaleidoscopic fall, and the short stormy days of winter. Nature is more real, closer, all around you, nudging. You can't help but notice.

When you live in the country, the causes and effects of our living on this earth are more noticeable, and things that urban dwellers take for granted are not necessarily entitlements. Water, you soon realize, does not always come from a pipe, at least not on its own. Country dwellers take on responsibility for their own needs in a physical sense that is not usually necessary, or even possible, in a city environment.

This book provides a guide for those who plan to live in the country. It outlines things to watch for when you are selecting country property, whether that property is already developed with a home or is raw land on which to build your dream place. The chapters on specifics like geographic area and climate will help you select where you will most enjoy your new country lifestyle. Other chapters cover access, title to real property, siting of improvements, and aspect of the land, without being technical.

The experiences of others who located in the country, taken from my twenty-five years of working in the real estate profession in southern Oregon, are chronicled to illustrate various points. The names of these people have been changed, but their stories are real. Though the individuals vary widely, their dreams are alike. The same yearnings for a simpler life have been voiced by person after person, couple after couple, both young families and retirees.

Concentrating on the search for a new home in which to live the country lifestyle is the theme of this book. Accordingly, emphasis is placed on what it means to live in the country, how to recognize what you're looking for when you see it, where you are most likely to find it, and how to go about the search. This book will help you plan the steps necessary to make your dreams a reality, by knowing what to expect and how to achieve your goals in the very different world that is the country.

1

Facilitating Your Change

John and Mary Jones were living in Los Angeles when they started looking for a retirement home in the countryside of southern Oregon. John had retired from a career in the military, where he had done a lot of research on climate. Several service publications carried data and rankings on various geographically diverse retirement areas. Studying these, they had come to the conclusion that the interior valleys of southwestern Oregon not only met their criteria, but had a lot to offer besides.

Since John and Mary planned to live an active retirement lifestyle and were not dependent on employment for their livelihood, their decision was an excellent one. They eventually purchased a sizable home on twenty acres about five miles from a town of fifteen thousand, where they had plenty of room to keep some animals if they desired. Their nearest neighbors were a quarter of a mile down the road, and it took them ten minutes to drive into town, where shopping was good and numerous cultural events took place.

John was eligible for veterans' health benefits, and the nearest VA hospital was just over one hundred miles away, a reasonable distance since the local medical community was sizable and equipped to handle any emergency. A four-year college was located nearby and a community college was an hour's drive away, facts that particularly interested Mary.

The Joneses had made the decision some time earlier to move to the country and take advantage of a more peaceful lifestyle. They had carefully researched the geographic location that would

1

be best for them. When the time came to purchase their country property, all that was left was to identify a specific property within that geographic area. The Joneses were unusual in that they had specific, well-defined dreams, making it easier to convert them into reality.

Many of us are not able to establish our criteria with such precision. We know only that the rat race has been getting us down and our anxiety level is up. We are approaching or experiencing burnout. Our big-city schools are a mess. Our tolerance for traffic, noise, confusion, pollution, and people has bottomed out. Finally we face these negative things that are so drastically affecting our lives and make a conscious decision to change them by moving to the country.

Once you have reached this point, what's next? Is there a logical order to implementing this decision?

The first step, unless you are financially independent, is to determine your source of income. Will you be depending on a job at your new location? Would you consider buying a business to operate for income?

MAKING A LIVING

Do not underestimate the importance of a certain income. The excitement of embarking on your dream to move to the country can overshadow proper attention to this vital matter. If the move is a retirement maneuver, income may be less important than if you are the breadwinner of a young family that will require ongoing financial support. In most rural areas, many jobs are part-time or low-key, dictated by the lower population density and resultant lesser demand. In those circumstances, retirees can often find supplemental employment, because a part-time or lower-income situation exactly fits their requirements.

Workers with construction trade skills are the most likely to find employment in their new rural location, regardless of the geographic area involved. Pure population growth (yes, even in the rural areas of the United States) sees to that. Many specific kinds of jobs may not be immediately available, however. Sometimes, because of extremely light populations spread over the rural areas of some states, being employed means some travel around the region or to the workplace. The bright side is that any such travel will likely be pleasant, without traffic difficulties.

Many high-tech companies are relocating into rural, small-town settings. There are several reasons for this. First, ownership of these companies tends to be environmentally sensitive. They recognize that their workforces will be most productive, most creative, if they can live and work in an area that complements this environmental awareness. Let those creative research-and-development types live by the river, ride a bicycle to work, look out of their lab and see nothing but nature, and the highest chance exists for inspiring genius. Offering a rural area for business and living can be a huge plus factor in competition for talented workers. Many companies have demonstrated this, and others are quickly following suit.

If you have skills in a high-tech field, you are very fortunate, because you can select from many different areas where you will be quickly employed.

If your profession is one with less demand, say, piano tuning, and you must stick by this skill either through desire or because of anxiety, you might want to reconsider the advisability of moving away from an area where sufficient population exists for there to be a need for tuning pianos. This caveat holds true for many similar specialty professions. If you are confident of your abilities, you may decide to make a move into an area where there is little or no demand for your skills, knowing that you can develop demand or create employment opportunities in any of several different ways. Many people have that kind of confidence, and it rarely betrays them.

Professionals in the medical field can develop a practice almost anywhere. Nurses are in demand. Professionals such as veterinarians, attorneys, CPAs, and others can usually find a niche in new locations, needing only to achieve reciprocity or pass the bar or board as required if moving to another state.

Counterpart factory jobs to those found in large cities may not exist in the rural scene. The same is true for some service industries. Service industry employment is presently the fastest-growing field in the country, however. Some of these opportunities are at living wage levels; others are at or close to minimum wage.

Many entrepreneurial people buy small businesses in rural areas and use that business an as income vehicle. This works well for some, probably those who would do well anyway, no matter where they decide to apply their talents. Many small rural businesses are of the "ma and pa" type, although chain or franchise stores and service industries are moving into the rural areas. There is no reason why an enterprising person cannot become one of those chain or franchise operators.

There are many people who have the attitude that no matter where they go, they will find something productive to do. Those fortunate folks will do just fine in rural areas.

Looking for a Job

Unfortunately for the new arrival, many of the jobs in rural areas are given first to the "good old boys," those who already live there. So what happens when you make an application to a local employer and reveal that you seek work as a condition to move into the area? Your chances drop dramatically, unless you just happen to be the answer to that employer's needs at that very instant, or unless you happen to have a rare, sought-after skill.

It stretches faith to the utmost to move to an area before you have secured employment, especially if that employment is extremely vital to you. This fact, more than any other, has prevented many aspiring families from moving to the country. But the fact is that probably more than half of the people who actually do move to the country do so on the faith that they will be able to survive there. A machinist might become an auto mechanic, an auto mechanic might work on heavy equipment. A retiree might drive a school bus, and a produce department manager might work at the local building supply and drive the transit mix concrete truck occasionally. The point is, for those with confidence, ability, and flexibility, there is a way.

Employment in small-town and rural areas is always highest when those areas are reasonably close to metropolitan population centers, say within one hundred miles. Unfortunately, the type of rural life found here is more hectic, more subject to metro bustle, than in those small towns that are far enough removed from population centers that no "bedroom community" pressures affect them. So there are trade-offs. The pure, unsophisticated, totally unaffected country area probably no longer exists in the United States. Rather, such areas are a blend—mostly country, but affected by population pressures and modernization, a part of our nation in growth and transition.

Conventional employment is found in the greatest quantity in and around metropolitan and urban areas. Opportunities diminish in direct proportion to the density of population, give or take special factors, as you move out from population centers into the rural areas farther than even the most staunch commuter can handle.

Such states as Nevada, except for the Las Vegas and Reno scene, do provide the kind of rustic western living that can be seen in old western movies. So do parts of California, Oregon, Washington, Idaho, Montana, the Dakotas, Utah, Wyoming, Colorado, Arizona, New Mexico, and parts of Texas. Many of the plains states also have large areas without population centers, where real country living still can be found. To a lesser degree, the same can be said of all the southern and eastern states, with the exception of population centers and the eastern seaboard. So it is possible to move to the country and really mean it, even in New York State.

Realize, though, that in the cattle country of eastern Nevada, for instance, you are going to be hard pressed to find employment of the conventional sort. In or around the small towns, maybe. But on the land itself? Not likely, unless you're a cowboy or rancher, and if you were, you wouldn't be reading a book about moving to the country. So if the wide open spaces of the West are calling you, make sure you know what they're saying.

SEED MONEY

Generally, the closer to a population center, the greater the value of real estate. So if you are moving from the city to the country and have a home to sell in the city, you will often receive a higher figure for this home than you will have to pay for a similar one in a small town. This is a supply-demand type of equation, one that usually holds true unless you make long-distance changes of geographic areas. A move to the country often means leaving a house on a tiny lot, with the idea of acquiring a home on acreage. The value of the acreage can raise the total value of the new residence up to or above that of the old.

In some cases, particularly where a move is made from a populated, high-living-standard area into a lightly populated region, as in leaving one of the metro areas in California for the Pacific Northwest, the value differential is sizable—and favorable. Homes like those that regularly sell for hundreds of thousands of dollars in Silicon Valley, for instance, can be found for as little as one-fourth that amount in many of the rural areas of the Northwest. This factor provides lots of funding for a country home project, with resources left over to last a year or two, even after Uncle Sam gets done with the transaction.

Unfortunately, a move from the populated East Coast into the Pacific Northwest may find values there as high as, or higher than, those found on the eastern seaboard. The favorable weather factor and livability of the West Coast brought about this differential decades ago. Similar disparities exist in other parts of our country.

There are lots of ways to determine values. Simply calling a chamber of commerce in a town near any area of interest will bring a flood of real estate ads, from which you can determine general value levels.

The most common way to finance your move to the country is by selling your present home. There are others: You may have savings. You may have a retirement plan from which you can secure funds. You may be able to borrow from an annuity, life insurance, or trust of which you are the owner or beneficiary. More and more these days, parents or other relatives help young people become established, a phenomenon spawned by rapid growth in the value of real estate that is outstripping the growth rate of the average worker's earning power.

Joe and Madeline Arnos were sitting in my real estate office after we returned from looking at a country property. The property consisted of a small but well-built home, flanked by large trees at the rear, with a drive approaching from the paved county road across three acres of pasture. This open pasture allowed a fantastic view of the Cascade mountains in the near distance. The previous owner had constructed a pond on the five-acre property, and while we were there, a flight of wild ducks had landed on the smooth surface.

Joe and Madeline were beside themselves. I could tell the minute they laid eyes on the place that we had matched their dreams with physical reality. Joe was an X-ray technician and could easily find employment at any of three local hospitals. But they did not own their own home. Their savings account did not contain enough for the required down payment. To them, it looked as if their dream property was beyond reach. While I was enumerating a number of possible sources of additional funds in hopes of discovering an asset they had not considered, Joe suddenly stopped me and turned to Madeline.

"What about your aunt Mary?" he asked.

Within minutes Madeline was on the phone, and it turned out that Aunt Mary had indeed put aside a sizable sum for Madeline. When the aunt learned of their need for funds to use as a down payment, she wisely concluded that a portion of the inheritance would provide needed help right now, and while she was there to enjoy giving it. Joe and Madeline started living their country dream.

Apart from the financial ability to purchase a country place, the question of a sustaining income is undoubtedly the most important aspect of making a move to the country. Failing to achieve that income, some move back into the city grind they hated, finding that it is even more distasteful now after they have experienced the more relaxed lifestyle.

Nevertheless, most people who are motivated strongly enough to make the break with an unsatisfactory lifestyle, and embrace a new one in the country, do so in spite of the obstacles. They adapt and make do. They change their line of work or strike out on their own in some endeavor. They are survivors. They fit in with the somehow simpler values of country living. They contribute to their new community in many ways, such as bringing new skills and enthusiastic attitudes and new appreciations. Their standard of living may have dropped by metropolitan measures, but exchanging clutter for space, hurry for relaxation, artificial for real makes it all worthwhile.

DETERMINING JOB POTENTIAL

• Consider those country areas where your skills are marketable

• Assess your ability to change your line of work

• Research job potential in your area of choice

• Consider buying a job—purchasing and running a small business

• Remember that with computers and fax machines, some work can be done anywhere

It is not unusual to find families living in the country but working in the city. This is the factor that leads to urban sprawl around metropolitan centers. In search of the good life, families move a bit farther out, but growth soon surrounds them, and they must again move farther out or be satisfied with their existing lifestyle. This scenario is played out millions of times. But do the participants really live in the country?

More than likely, the type of property available to them at the end of that long commute is a subdivision, with similar homes on small lots, surrounded by more of the same. Though initially that residential development may have been in the country, by definition the country was lost the minute the development took place. Little is gained by the move, except possibly slightly lower property values and often new schools that will become crowded within a few years.

But often this scenario of living in the country and working in the city can be made to work. The determining factor can be the size of the city involved. If your employment is in a large metropolitan area, you will find real country living within commuting range only if you are very lucky. Generally speaking, your luck will be much better in the eastern portion of the country than in the West.

If your employment can be supported in a medium-size city, it is often possible to find a country haven within a reasonable distance. In this enviable arrangement, the country lifestyle is possible without giving up the higher earnings of big-city employment. If the employment and the commute to it are tolerable, this situation works.

All who dream of living the country life fit in somewhere between the commuter who lives in the suburbs and works in a high rise and the cowboy who may not see even a tiny town for weeks at a time.

2

To Build or to Buy?

There are basically two ways to acquire a country home. The first is to purchase an existing home in the country, and the second is to build a new one. Either decision may be right for you, or make sense because of conditions in the area where you have decided to locate. Factors that affect your decision are highly individual, but often looking objectively at this choice can be extremely helpful. There are four main areas to consider when making your decision: cost, time, availability, and aesthetics.

COST COMPARISON FACTORS
Country real estate prices reflect the inflation of recent years. But depending upon geographic area, the effects of inflation do not always apply equally to the two components of a country home: land and improvements. Thus there may be financial advantages to consider in making a decision to either buy an existing home in the country or build your dream home.

In most desirable areas, land has appreciated at a more rapid rate than the cost of improvements. This is because the land is finite—no more of it is being created, at least at a rate that is meaningful. So as the demand for country living sites increases in good climate regions, the value of land increases at the same rate or faster.

Improvements on the land (such as a home) do not continue to grow more valuable at the same rate as the land does. A long-standing theory holds that buildings depreciate as they grow older and components either wear out or become outdated. For

9

this reason, in many areas you could probably purchase a fifteen-hundred-square foot home, twenty years old, on five acres, for less than you could purchase the same property if the home were newly built.

Though the value of a home is being lowered by depreciation, that value is also increasing because of the inflationary increase in the cost of building a comparable home today. Because the increase in the cost of construction of a comparable home is greater than the loss of value of an existing home through depreciation, the net effect on the home is that the market value increases. Nevertheless, the total value of an existing home (land and building costs minus depreciation) still lags behind the total cost of building new, which may make purchase of an existing home a comparative bargain.

Many other factors contribute to the often higher cost of building new. Many building codes have been refined in recent years, especially in the areas of energy conservation and safety. These changes have caused the costs of residential building to rise. Some of the added costs are recoverable over time (energy-saving devices should eventually pay for themselves, for example), but other costs are not. Modern building codes offer very high living standards in most new housing. This may or may not be what you're looking for. But if you decide to build new, you can do little but comply with current standards whether you want all of them or not.

The depletion of public-land timber resources (which have long subsidized building and the housing market) has had a noticeable effect on the cost of new construction. Other conservation measures may limit the availability of land or raise the cost of a wide variety of materials.

If you purchase a new home that was built for sale on a country site, you will pay one price. If you find and purchase your land and hire a contractor to build a new home for you, you may well pay a different price, even if the homes are similar in size and details. If you act as your own contractor, and deal directly with subcontractors and tradesmen to build that new home yourself, it is likely that the final costs will differ yet again, and probably end up being less.

An especially exciting aspect of moving to the country is the opportunity to build a home and do the work yourself. As your experience increases and skills grow, your building project will progress faster and be more fun. Help for inexperienced builders is available from building departments, building material dealers, and do-it-yourself books. As a rule, the more individual operations, such as cabinetry, flooring, wiring, and plumbing that you can do yourself, the greater the savings will be. Roughly speaking, half of the cost of a new home is attributable to labor.

If you have not had experience in building or related fields, and if learning these new skills seems impossible to you, take a careful approach. How do you feel about a task of this magnitude? Do you thrive on overcoming adversity? Will you enjoy the challenges involved, or will building responsibilities create unbearable stress? These are questions that each individual must answer before making the decision to do the actual construction himself.

TIME CONSIDERATIONS
If you buy an existing home, possession and move-in can be as soon as a month or even less. The average is a somewhat longer period, but still very rapid compared to building a new home on acreage.

Depending upon weather, construction peak times, what month construction begins, and similar considerations, building a new home in the country can take from four or five months to as long as a year. If you wish to live in the area prior to that time, renting or some other temporary living arrangement is necessary. Some new country residents live on their land in an RV while they or their contractor build the home.

AVAILABILITY
Demand is greatest in those areas where living is good in terms of climate, services, employment, and other factors. Demand may make availability of large numbers of country homes and acreages unlikely where you will be searching. Or, there may be a fairly large number of small acreages available while existing country homes are at a premium. Or the case may be reversed. In these instances, the decision whether to buy existing or build new can be influenced by which is most advantageous in the region.

If there are many existing country homes available, not only is there a greater possibility that you will find one you like, but competition between sellers (a slow market) may enable you to purchase at a lower price. And if small acreages are scarce, demand for them may elevate values. In this case purchasing an existing home may be far less costly than purchasing a premium acreage and building. Conversely, if acreages are plentiful and existing homes scarce, it is likely that these circumstances will work in reverse, and you may be able to build new at the same total cost involved had you purchased an existing home.

Land use controls in some areas have severely limited the number of small acreages that can be developed. In this case, not only will there be few choices of unimproved country sites, but those that can be built on will have a high value. In such regions purchasing an existing country home may be the only way to locate there—but demand and a fixed supply may have increased the value of those existing homes.

AESTHETICS

In areas of the country where demand is great, the most desirable sites may have already been developed with homes. Examples would include small acreages that front on a lake or running water, view bluffs, or nestle in wooded knolls with good views. These types of country sites appeal to many people and usually are developed early in the country growth pattern. In rural areas where such sites are limited and demand high, purchasing one of the existing homes on such a site may by the only alternative if that type of site is what you are seeking.

If you do find a site on which to build your home, the way the house looks and whether it fits into the environment are all within your control. You can select natural materials that blend with nature, and design features that look at home in the country. You will get exactly what you want. There will be few trade-offs in suitability for your lifestyle, and your home will reflect your values and your personality. When you purchase an existing home, though, you inherit the results of the taste of the person who created that home. If that taste matches yours, well and good. If it doesn't, you will either have to learn to live with it or plan to change it by remodeling now or in the future.

3

Defining Your Dreams

Can you describe your dream? Can you put it in terms of hills and valleys, lakes and streams, field and forest, lanes and rustic homes? Can you see views in the distance of snow-capped peaks or plains, of fields with horses or livestock, of a garden, or of children walking? Do you envision a home of logs, or rustic wood, or contemporary but nestled at the side of a knoll, blending in with nature? What does your total dream look like? And equally important, if not more so, where is your dream located? Of all the geographic regions in the United States, where will you be happiest? To answer this, you need to consider several factors.

PRIORITIES
- Services
- Schools
- Culture
- Geography
- Demographics
- Climate
- Recreation

The sum total of the above priorities existing in an area determine the dominant lifestyle there. Putting the face of reality on your dream not only can be extremely helpful in recognizing the dream when it appears, but also will be a strong step toward actual fulfillment.

To help you define your dream, list your priorities as you envision them in your new lifestyle. How important are the services you now take for granted? Now, just a short trip will take you to all kinds of shopping. Food and food specialties, dry goods in your choice of dozens of discount or warehouse stores, upper-bracket stores that display and stock the best of everything are all conveniently close. Whatever you are looking for is stocked in some store or business, even consumer goods so obscure that the market is very narrow. All manner of specialty services can be summoned by a phone call. This is one of the benefits of a metropolitan area—a benefit you will probably be leaving behind.

Those specialty service industries in metropolitan areas exist because there is sufficient demand in metro populations. There will be auto repair shops in almost every community, because the need is universal and sufficient to support that type of business, but it is unlikely that you will find a professional in a small town to tune your piano.

The loss of services as you move to the country is not an absolute, every-time trade-off, but it is generally part of the country equation. For this reason, it is helpful to honestly decide how important these frills are to you. For most country dwellers, many services are available within less than a one-day drive. This drive is made every six months by some, and once a month or more frequently by others. In many cases, metropolitan availability for goods and services is but two or three hours away.

With this in mind, you can decide for yourself what importance immediate availability of goods has for you. It will then become easier to evaluate country areas based on this consideration. If you are loath to give up handy proximity to every conceivable type of goods and service, then you will want to relocate to an area where these amenities are available within a distance that is tolerable for you.

Schools in country areas and smaller towns can provide an educational atmosphere that is often missing in larger cities. One reason is that the school system receives higher participation from parents within each district. In many areas, districts are small and manageable. Small-town schools, often also small in numbers of students, can fulfill their educational functions without having to divert resources to combat such elements as organized gangs, deteriorating neighborhoods, or a myriad of other problems.

When children are raised in a country environment, a different attitude toward school and the pursuit of an education is often present. Teachers are able to inspire and provide an environment in which the students become motivated. Some indications of this in rural schools are lower percentages of dropouts and higher percentages of students continuing on to college. The ratio of students per teacher is often more favorable in rural school districts, which may account for some of the successes. Teachers also feel more supported by parents and residents in the district when that district is small, and most people know each other.

There are several ways to investigate educational facilities in a small community. Contacting an active member of the PTA will give you one perspective of school district operations. Contacting the district itself will likely give another. School board members are generally very knowledgeable about most aspects of the school operation. Parents of children attending the school will always have opinions about their particular school, which may or may not be valid. If you get the same comments from a number of parents, it is likely that some reason for the concurrence exists. Consider talking to several of the teachers from the school in which you are interested. You will learn a lot about their job satisfaction, which tells you whether those teachers are being helped to perform their jobs.

Consider contacting the high school to learn about students' SAT scores. Data about college entrance applications, as well as the percentage of students from that high school who have attended college, are indicators of the success of primary and secondary education in the local schools.

Cultural advantages are often important. Clara and John came into my office one day in May. It was easy to see that they were perplexed, and upon talking to them, the reason became apparent. Clara was obviously the one in charge in their relationship, although both of them wanted to begin living a relaxed, country lifestyle. Like so many, they were fleeing the southern California rat race.

Clara was a teacher and an organizer. She was able to verbalize about their dream, and described a home along the banks of a stream, far from neighbors, where about the only thing they would hear was wind in the pines. They had found such a property two days before, and this was the cause of their uncertainty. The property they had found was located in eastern Oregon, far out in arid country where there is a lot of beauty but virtually no population.

Clara and John had found the physical part of their dream, but it was in the wrong place. Clara intended to seek employment teaching at the high school level. In addition, she had a strong interest in literature and the theater. If Clara and John located in eastern Oregon, they would be thirty miles from the nearest high school, a very small facility with no employment openings. They would be more than one hundred miles from the nearest institution of higher learning, which was trade school oriented. Since our small town boasted a four-year college, and also happened to be the Shakespearean center of the United States, the match was easy. I showed them a property about ten miles out in the country that came close to what they had described to me. That property did not have the same wild beauty and pristine aura as the one they had inspected in eastern Oregon, but the necessary benefits were there. The total package fit. Clara and John are still happy with their move today, ten years later. Would Clara have been happy isolated out in the wide open spaces? How long would the wild beauty of the remote location have been enough to satisfy them? Locating in a county where the population was 150,000 people, and the amenities they were seeking existed, was a far wiser choice.

The presence of cultural advantages and events is strong evidence in determining whether there are other people in the area who have these interests. The existence of theater groups or local playhouses, art galleries, and opera or symphony performances are good indicators that the community values culture. If these things are important to you, make sure they are available.

Geographic features also can be very important. A man named John from Nebraska was looking for a retirement home in the forest. I had sent him photographs of a beautiful rustic home in the mountains, nestled in a grove of tall, green conifers. I picked John up at the airport, and we began the twenty-minute drive up into the mountains. John grew silent, then he paled and would not look out of the car as we climbed higher above the valley. John could not tolerate the topography. The hillside that sloped from the highway down to the valley below absolutely terrified him. We never reached the property. I learned a lesson, and so did John.

Some people are turned off by endless plains. Others believe they would be happiest on the coast where they can watch the endless waves of the restless ocean. But they also must adequately assess the effects of fog and rainfall, common coastal phenomena. And those who are drawn to living in the high elevations need to honestly determine how they will react to snow, for snow there will be, lots of it, and for months at a time. Will it still be thrilling after the novelty wears off?

The best way to determine how the geography of an area affects you is to go there. If that is impractical, a library can suggest research resources that will be helpful. You also can inquire of local institutions or chambers of commerce.

Information on the populations of rural areas and the economics that support that population is also readily available from local chambers of commerce. From this data you can determine if a specific area has the features you want, and how accessible those features will be to you as you live your new country lifestyle.

Library research and inquiries to chambers of commerce in areas of interest are also good ways to learn about what living in an area is really like. Remember, though, that chamber of commerce data is always slanted to put the best countenance upon the area. Climate will be described in positive phrases. Temperatures will often be expressed as averages. Find out the coldest and hottest temperatures. Remember that a low of 0 degrees and a high of 120 degrees average out to a balmy 60 degrees, not an accurate indication of your comfort level.

Rainfall, snowfall, and prevailing winds are just as important as temperature when it comes to evaluating a climate for enjoyable living. Even if temperatures and precipitation are within reasonable limits, will you enjoy outdoor living if the prevailing wind blows thirty miles an hour 180 days of the year?

Good climate data can be secured from the various weather stations operated by the federal weather bureau, the National Oceanic and Atmospheric Administration (NOAA). Listings can be found in the library, in phone books and other publications, for the nearest station to the area you are investigating.

How important are recreational opportunities in your plan?

Often the dream of moving to the country is interwoven with a dream of the great outdoors. Hiking, skiing, snowmobiling, fishing, being out in natural places—these all have an allure for many people. There are recreation opportunities available everywhere, but those activities may not be high on your list of preferences. If your recreation preferences involve the ocean and you locate in Wyoming, you will be severely limited. You will feel the same limitations if you aspire to hike in the mountains and locate near a small town in Kansas. So think about the importance of recreation in your life, and factor this into your geographic investigation. Since you are making a lifestyle change, include as many advantages as you can.

SOME PROPERTY TYPES AND THEIR USES

- Agricultural
    1. Livestock
    2. Crops
- Forest
    1. Aesthetics
    2. Commercial
- Recreational
    1. Waterfront
    2. Forest
    3. Adjoining public land
- Fringe properties at the edge of town
- In town
- Business
    1. In small town
    2. In country or recreation area

Most country properties will fit somewhere within the above categories. Regardless of the type of environment you desire for your home and living experience, it is definable in terms of form and shape. If you can visualize or picture that form and shape, your search for your dream property will be more successful. What does it look like physically? Is it a rustic home under trees, on the shore of a small lake? Or is it a staunch, weathered cottage on a bluff at the seashore? Does it stand in a meadow, flanked by cottonwoods, with a view of forest, beyond which are brilliant, shimmering snowcaps? Or do you see pasture, fences, maybe a barn, with space for a few farm animals to give your children a taste of the real country? Maybe it is a modest home in a friendly neighborhood in a small town, where all the neighbors not only know each other, but like each other as well.

Agricultural Properties

Agricultural properties are those that have as a basic purpose the production of something from the land. Such properties are usually income producing. The production of income does not necessarily guarantee the making of a profit, however. This is an often overlooked distinction.

Agricultural properties may be anything from a few acres to thousands of acres in size. They are of two basic types, one primarily involving the raising of livestock or other animals, and the other the growing of crops, which are then marketed. Chicken ranches, rabbitries, horse farms, cattle ranches, llama farms, and other exotic enterprises such as ostrich raising are some examples of the first type of agricultural property, where the final purpose of the endeavor is to produce animals. On a five-acre property, if most of the land is irrigated, raising animals can be a productive use if properly managed. The income from such a small operation will usually be relatively insignificant, however, except with enterprises such as chicken or egg farms, where large numbers of livestock can be raised on a small amount of land.

At the other extreme are large cattle ranches of relatively poor land, where dozens of acres are required to raise one cow. Here physical size can run into tens of thousands of acres to enable the rancher to raise a few hundred head of cattle. Romantic and reeking of the Old West? Certainly. Profitable? Maybe. Livestock operations like this are mostly on a paying basis only for those who inherited the land or purchased it long ago at a lower cost level. The demand for rural land today is such that values have risen in many regions to the point where it is not economical to ranch the land. The value of the total investment at current levels is greater than the income that can be produced from the livestock operation.

Examples of the second type of agricultural property, enterprises that grow plants in the soil, are vineyards, fruit or berry farms, nurseries, grain ranches, and row crop farms. As with other types of agriculture, specialty knowledge is required if such enterprises are to be economically productive.

Hans Schoon, his wife, and their four young children came into my office in response to an advertisement featuring a country home on four acres of irrigated land. Hans confided that he wanted to make his living from whatever property he finally purchased. I tried to deflate his dream gently, to get him in touch with economic reality by suggesting that he could supplement his income with that property, but he would undoubtedly have to work at a job in the area. I added that living on that property, where his children could have animals and enjoy the country lifestyle, was probably the major benefit. Hans bought the place in spite of my caveat.

What I didn't know was that Hans had great experience raising berries. Before long, strawberries, raspberries and others that I didn't know existed flourished on the property. With their children helping, the Schoons soon had a very profitable, albeit very labor intensive, operation in full swing. Hans did take a job during the winter months when the berry farm was dormant, but I suspect he didn't need to. Soon the family put up a stand and retailed their produce to local people. The Schoon farm was a success because of the special knowledge that made it possible to raise a highly specialized crop and the availability of family labor to operate what was a very completely farmed four acres.

Most seekers of country life find that a few acres of land is more than enough to give them a taste of farming or ranching. On a few acres of pasture, a number of head of livestock can be raised, along with a horse or two for the kids. The result will not be a significant income; your profit will probably be something like a continuous supply of free beef, with enough left over to sell and pay the property taxes. If children are involved, the lifestyle experience will be extremely memorable and will provide that great benefit: They will have been raised in the country.

Sylvan Properties

Many people wish to live in or near wooded areas. It is not surprising that most sitings of rural homes in the trees are done for aesthetic reasons. There is something about the sighing of a gentle afternoon breeze in the needles of a conifer or the peaceful undulations of deciduous leaves that instills feelings of contentment in the observer. Trees stand strong against wind and storm, models of stability under adversity. In the spring they burst with new life and growth, giving us a sense of renewal.

Sometimes the trees themselves become the building materials, as with log or timber frame homes. A log home at the edge of a clearing in a few acres of tall conifers, landscaped with natural plantings, looks like it grew there. That same log home on a building lot in town next to a contemporary home would look out of place.

In a few cases, living on a forest property is profitable because the property is being actively managed as a tree farm. Such activity may involve reforestation, thinning, and eventually, selective harvest of forest species.

Recreational Properties

This broadest of categories could conceivably include most other types of real property. A fishing cabin and a ski chalet in the mountains are recreational properties, as are homes on the lake, at the seashore, and in any other location where the primary intent is to provide access to recreational pursuits. Most of us think of recreational property as a second home used intermittently for vacation purposes. Certainly most second homes qualify as recreational, as do many homes purchased for retirement. But many people live close to recreational facilities, which they use nearly every day, year-around.

Sometimes the attractive feature of a property is that it adjoins huge areas of public land, which in effect opens up vast acreages for hiking, exploring, and other outdoor activities. Such properties can be classified as clearly recreational, especially for the owner who is interested in the amenities the public land access provides.

Fringe Properties

Fringe properties are those located in that area from the town limits outward until reasonable driving distance is exceeded, and these are the areas to which most people moving to the country tend to gravitate. Nearly every other classification of property type will be found here; the distinction is one of location.

The fringe areas are where school buses operate on country roads. Parents taxi children to 4-H meetings and other functions. Usually town is less than a fifteen- or twenty-minute drive away, a compromise between life in the boondocks (the "real" country) and life in the small town. Homes on small acreages abound on the fringes, especially close to town. As distance from the town limits increases, so does the size of the land parcels. This is true no matter what the type or usage of the land.

In Town
Perhaps few will set out initially to locate in town. Generally, though, the availability of property is greater in town than in the country, and real estate values may be lower in small towns than for a comparable home on acreage out in the fringe areas. Services are available and handy. It is possible, and safe, to walk to shopping and other activities.

An in-town property usually consists of a home on a residential lot. Because of travel when living out in the fringe area, as well as cost of utilities and fire insurance, living in a small town today is often less expensive. Another factor is the financing preference for homes in town over country homes generally shown by lenders. It is not unusual for much larger down payments to be required for country properties.

Businesses
The ma and pa business is not dead, but it is seriously ill, victim to several factors not the least of which is the franchised or chain operation. From auto parts to hamburgers, franchised operations are a form of small business that has great acceptance and is here to stay. Buying a franchise may be a viable option for the enterprising city escapee who is capable and willing to run a small business instead of securing employment. In many small-town areas, however, most of the small businesses available on the market are still the ma and pa type. Often such businesses have been operating at the same location for many years. In these communities, local reputation is vital, and so is the service the owner provides.

Regardless of the type of business, a new purchaser is buying a vehicle on which to place her or his efforts and make money. Experience with the type of business, personality of the operator, available trade, and other factors all have a bearing on how successful the business will be. It is not unusual for new competition from small shopping centers to adversely impact the existing older businesses, which are often located out of the newer traffic patterns.

Sometimes the business location includes living facilities. This is true for those who operate such businesses as a fishing resort on the lake or a small-town motel. The business may be located in the country, such as a small country grocery or feed store. Other enterprises are in or near town, such as retail facilities, small-town shopping malls or centers, and apartment complexes.

4

Access: Can You Get There?

Harvey J. was hopping mad. He could hardly talk when he first walked into the office. I didn't know why he had come to see me. I hadn't sold him the forty acres of wooded land that he had owned for a year now; another broker had made that sale. But here was Harvey, with a case of tight jaws.

"I came down from Portland today, and I can't get to my property!" he complained. "There's a locked gate across the road."

I knew that I couldn't help Harvey. He needed legal advice. But to make him feel better, I listened to his story. He had not visited his acreage since purchasing it a year ago, when he was transported there by a salesperson. When he tried to drive to the acreage today, he encountered a locked gate where "his" access road turned off from the county road. Harvey had a problem.

I knew some of the history of the access to Harvey's property. The road that led to his forty acres crossed land that was owned by another party. The road had been built a number of years ago to haul out logs that were cut on Harvey's land. There were no improvements on the land, which had previously been owned by a party from another state who rarely visited.

I suspected that the right-of-way for that road had expired when the logging was completed, but I didn't tell Harvey. I referred him to a local attorney. If he was lucky, he could buy a right-of-way for his road at a reasonable cost. If not, he would be involved in lengthy and expensive litigation attempting to obtain access to his own land.

It is extremely important as a purchaser of rural property to know that you have access to that property. Often, even the owner does not understand the finer points of access, especially in cases where the property in question has no buildings or improvements and has not been lived on.

Right-of-way and access statutes vary from state to state. In some states, access cannot be readily denied and there are laws set up defining how that access will be allowed. In other states, a property can exist and property taxes be paid on it, but all the while there is no legal, rightful way to get there. That condition is often referred to as *landlocked*.

When a property touches a public road—that is, a boundary of the property is a common boundary with that public road—the property is considered to have frontage on that road, and access is usually implied. The frontage must, however, extend far enough to physically allow for an access driveway. Five feet of frontage will not suffice for a road ten feet wide to accommodate a six-foot-wide vehicle. But other cautions need to be observed. Most county roads, and certain state highways, have access requirements and sometimes restrictions.

Access is often limited on roads where the sight distance is impaired, as on a sharp corner. If an oncoming vehicle cannot see another vehicle pulling onto the roadway in time to stop, then no private access is allowed at that point for safety reasons.

For other traffic safety considerations, some state highways limit the number of accesses along a given distance. Sometimes frontage roads paralleling the highway provide access, but in many cases they do not. Even when a property has frontage on an existing public road, access is not guaranteed.

When you move to the country, your home will probably not be located on a busy road, but on a country lane or even on your own private road. And here legal access becomes less certain. If the country lane has been dedicated to the public and accepted by the political subdivision (city, county, or borough) in which it is located, that lane probably qualifies as legal access. But to be certain, you must check with local authorities or have a local title company run a search on the status of the lane.

Sometimes a truly gorgeous spot will be located far from any county road and reached by a secondary road that may or may not be heavily used. Who maintains this road? If you are in a region with winter snow, who plows the snow? Is there a deeded right-of-way for the road? Is the property one of those that the road right-of-way was deeded to serve? It is possible to find a property that abuts on a private roadway (has frontage) but has no legal right to use that roadway because the property was not granted right-of-way on the private road. Situations of this kind can become involved.

There is a type of access referred to in many states as *prescriptive*. A prescriptive easement is perfected when a specified route has been used for access continually for a certain period of years. If this access has never been disturbed or contested, the right to use that access has probably been legally established, regardless of whether the route crosses land belonging to others. This is *prescriptive access* or a *prescriptive easement*. Though in most states the party using the access would likely prevail if others attempted to block that access, litigation would be involved until the matter was adjudicated (ruled on by the court). So prescriptive access is not proof against attempts to block that access, because it is not deeded, or written, until adjudicated.

Prescriptive access usually cannot be upgraded. If you purchase property where the prior owner used a prescriptive easement to go in and cut firewood on the land once a year, you receive that same access right. Trouble may be brewing if you attempt to upgrade that prescriptive right by increasing the frequency of use to daily, as would be necessary if you were considering living on the land.

The question of access is very touchy, and it is critical when considering country property. Though in nearly every case access can eventually be secured through the courts, the process is not only lengthy, but extremely costly. The uncertainty and frustration that such action inevitably creates take their toll. Not the least of complications in access fights is the real possibility that your adversary may be your closest neighbor.

What steps should be taken by the prudent buyer of country property to make sure there is access to that property? If you are buying directly from an owner, the entire burden of checking out access is directly on you; you cannot rely on what the present owner tells you. If you are purchasing through a real estate agency, the agency will provide some expertise and help. Even so, to be certain of access, you will have to do some verification for yourself.

The easiest, safest, and often least expensive way to deter-

provided. There is a charge for such information, which involves a search of records kept either at the county courthouse or at the title company itself.

A road's status must be determined, even if the road is in constant and heavy use by many residents for whom it provides access. The longer the distance traveled on such a road, the more important ownership of the road becomes, because of the need for upkeep and repair of the road.

Many properties located on private roads have legal access over those roads. This condition usually occurs when the road was built to serve as access for those properties fronting on it. Legal access is created by an easement document, which specifically deeds access rights to certain properties. But the questions still remain of who owns the land on which the road is located and who pays the property taxes on that land. How the road is maintained is often spelled out in an agreement or in the easement document itself. Maintenance responsibility is often shared equally by the users or apportioned by some formula. Without a maintenance agreement, disagreements or different perceptions of proper upkeep can cause friction among the users.

If a private road used for access to your property is gated, or locked, find out why this is the case, especially if you are the only party using the portion beyond the gate. You may find that you will have to continually lock and unlock the gate as you come and go from your property.

Sometimes, especially in the case of unimproved acreage, there is no road to the land at all. This would be the case if the property is being parceled or divided from the rear portion of an existing larger acreage. In some cases, access is provided by a deeded easement to such a parcel. In other cases, a deeded strip of land that is part of the acreage is included for the purpose of road access. This strip leads out to and touches a public roadway, thus providing the frontage for access. Such parcels are called *flag lots,* the "flagstaff" being the long, narrow strip of deeded land intended for road access.

A number of rural sites, especially in the western states, are reached by roadways that were built by, and are located on land owned by, federal land management agencies, primarily the U.S. Forest Service and the Bureau of Land Management. Many states retain ownership of various classes of resource lands, often in trust as school endowments, and nearby private lands are reached by crossing these state lands. If the property you are interested in is reached by such a road, contact the agency having jurisdiction to find out whether the road may be used as legal access to private property and whether the administering agency maintains the road and, if so, to what standards. This is especially important in areas where winter snow must be plowed.

Some country properties are actually islands or portions of islands. Most such islands are located in inland lakes or rivers, but in some instances the islands are surrounded by salt water. If the distance is short enough, island access may be by bridge. Otherwise, the property must be reached by boat. If this is the case, find out if there is a public or deeded area from which to launch and moor your vessel on the mainland side. The right to boat freely on the water must be available. Most water that has been adjudicated as "navigable" is freely open to the public for boating. Also consider access when and if the water freezes.

Whether you are buying directly from a seller or through a real estate agency, it is imperative in the purchase of country property that you learn the facts regarding legal access to the property in which you are interested.

◆

5

Water

Whether your country dream calls for finding a home already built or you long to create your own home on that exactly right piece of acreage, water is an important consideration. As soon as you decide to live outside municipalities, or areas that may also be served by water districts organized as public utilities, securing water becomes an individual responsibility. Some country developments have organized and built waterworks that serve small-acreage owners within compact areas. Generally, however, country residents must provide for their own water.

Among common sources for domestic water, or water for household use, are wells, springs, streams or water flows, lakes, ponds, and stored seasonal runoff water. With some variation, these are the same sources used, often in combination, for municipal water supplies.

Wells are a common means of accessing underground water. Drilled, bored, driven, or even hand dug, depending on location and local conditions, wells tap water in underground aquifers. These aquifers may be underground reservoirs or pools, occupying space in sand, gravel, or other rock, or they may be underground, slowly moving streams, sometimes small with very light flow through crevices and faults in bedrock.

In some geographic areas, well drillers can estimate accurately the depth necessary to secure adequate water. This is because other wells drilled in the immediate vicinity indicate the presence of water at a certain depth. In other areas, no such uniformity exists and the depths of wells vary. Variations also may be present in the yield and quality of water from the wells.

Strict standards for drinking-water quality have been established by the federal government. Nearly all municipal water systems treat the water before releasing it into water mains for distribution. Treatment ranges from mechanical, to remove particles in suspension, to chemical, to remove excess minerals and kill bacterial and viral pollution.

Only a small portion of individual water systems involve water treatment. One reason is that there are few requirements for testing domestic water for individual residential usage. The most common treatment is water softening, used in hard-water areas mainly to remove excess calcium. Iron in undesirable quantities is often a problem with well and spring water. Filters are available that will reduce iron content to acceptable levels. Chlorinators are also commonly in use where bacterial pollution is present on a permanent or intermittent basis. Both water softeners and chlorinators are relatively inexpensive for individual systems, although they require periodic servicing. Several other types of filters available for home use further remove certain impurities from the water, including the chlorine used for initial treatment.

Somewhat recently, drinking-water purity has become an issue. The EPA has set minimum standards for drinking water supplied by municipal systems. To varying degrees, these standards may be applied to individual domestic water systems by local or state regulatory agencies. Besides hardness (usually caused by dissolved calcium), which easily can be removed by water conditioners, there may be standards for allowable manganese, acidity, alkalinity, salinity, nitrates, and turbidity. Treatments are available to bring any one of these offending conditions to within allowable limits.

Newly recognized as a problem, and the subject of much publicity and many warnings on recreational water supplies on public lands, is a cyst called *Giardia lamblia*. Presence of this parasite in rural surface water supplies cannot be dismissed lightly. Disinfecting the water with chlorine, allowing for sufficient time between water treatment and use, is one cure for *Giardia* infestation.

Perhaps the majority of country residences use wells as their source of domestic water. Though the initial cost of drilling the

This 700-foot ditch will carry a water pipeline from a well to the residence and electricity from the residence to the well. A longer distance from the building site to the well adds to building costs, but possible well sites closer to the residence did not hold the promise of adequate water.

well and installing a pump is substantial, once completed there is usually little maintenance. A submersible pump is installed down in the well itself, safe from freezing in low winter temperatures. Such pumps are economical, requiring lower-horsepower motors than the centrifugal jet pump, which is installed on the top of the well.

When purchasing a country property serviced by a well, it is important to determine the flow or yield of the well. Some counties or states enforce statutes that require well tests upon change of ownership of the property. Pump companies test wells by attaching their metering equipment and letting the pump run for a given period of time, measuring the amount of water produced. The flow is usually stated as the number of gallons produced per minute.

Springs, defined as a free flow of water from the ground, are

sometimes used as domestic water sources. Though the spring
water itself may be quite free of pollutants, care must be taken in
designing the collection works that guide the water flow into a
pipe in order to avoid contamination from outside sources. Even
if no domestic animals are present, small creatures such as mice
can be a source of *e. coli* bacteria and pollute the water. Typically,
the spring flow is collected in a storage tank before being fed into
a domestic system. If the spring location and storage are located
at an elevation sufficiently above the residence, a gravity flow system can be installed, requiring no electrical energy for pumps.
Fifty feet in elevation will provide approximately twenty pounds
per square inch of water pressure.

Domestic water from ponds or lakes usually is procured by
pumping from these water bodies at a depth free from surface
disturbance and contaminants. Water quality can vary widely,

Spring Development

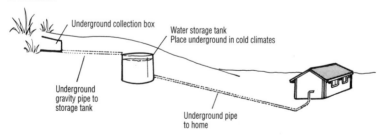

*Spring development can take many forms, some more complicated than
the simple system shown here. Where the spring is fifty feet or higher in
elevation above the home, a completely gravity flow system is possible.
Each foot of elevation creates approximately 0.4 pounds of pressure.*

and there can be problems during cold weather, especially if the lake or pond is shallow. Treatment of water from all such open sources is highly recommended.

Streams and rivers require pump installations similar to those on lakes or ponds. Fluctuating water flows, as well as turbidity during high-runoff periods, may require special design of pumping installations. Treatment of the water to assure purity is an absolute necessity.

Reservoirs that collect and store winter runoff water may be practical water sources under some conditions. A fairly large storage capacity and depths of a dozen or more feet are necessary. This source, while it should not be overlooked in areas where securing water is difficult, may present more problems than the other sources. Runoff water from micro watersheds, especially when that runoff is seasonal surface water, may contain excessive bacteria and viral contaminants. In addition, turbidity may be a problem and, depending on the cause, may not be removed completely by settling.

Cisterns that catch rainwater from roofs have a definite place in areas where water is extremely scarce. Often these areas do not have sufficient rainfall to make storage cisterns practical as an only source, but even a few inches of rain annually falling on a sizable roof can amount to many thousands of gallons. In some other areas, particularly where recently laid down volcanic soils are found, groundwater may be very difficult to obtain, even though annual precipitation is adequate. In such cases, cisterns to store roof runoff may be quite practical. Utilizing roof water in storage cisterns often requires a second water system within the residence that uses cistern water for such purposes as flushing toilets, where water of drinking quality is not required.

How Much Water Is Enough?

Lifestyle, more than any other single factor, determines how much water a household will use. Other factors are the number of people in the household and whether there is usage outside the home, such as watering a lawn or garden. Regular flush toilets use about five gallons of water each time they are flushed, and a bath or shower can consume twenty to forty gallons of water. Such modern conveniences as dishwashers, automatic clothes washers, and garbage disposals are large users of water, and if they will be used, the supply of water must accommodate them. If a large land-scaped area, especially a lawn, will be watered regularly, surprisingly greater water usage will occur.

Often lending institutions require well or water system flow tests on country wells and have established a minimum flow level in order to qualify for financing. In many areas, five gallons per minute is the required minimum flow. This is sufficient to run perhaps two small lawn sprinklers continuously, provided the well yield is also continuous. In a twenty-four-hour period, these two sprinklers will release seventy-two hundred gallons of water onto that lawn.

Many estimates of water usage have been advanced, among them the figure of four hundred gallons of water per day per person when all uses, indoors and out, are considered. At this rate, a three-person household will use twelve hundred gallons of water every twenty-four hours. This is only one-fifth of the production of a well that yields five gallons per minute.

Would a well yielding one gallon per minute be sufficient? To many well drillers, such a low-yield well is considered dry. If all the water can be used from a well with a yield of one gallon per minute, 1,440 gallons will be available every twenty-four hours. To utilize a low-yield well, the production must be regularly pumped and stored in tanks. Such a system then makes use of a second pressure pump system, drawing from the storage tanks. High-gallon usage for short periods of time is then accommodated by drawing upon the stored water.

Similar storage tanks can be used when a low-yield spring is the water source. Storage capacity should be sufficient for a two- or three-day supply. Tanks can be of any nontoxic material. Wood, steel, concrete, and plastic are generally used for water storage tanks. Placing storage tanks underground serves both to keep the water cool and to protect the system from freezing in areas with cold winters.

Low-yield sources, then, can provide more than sufficient supplies of water if the yield is stored as it is produced. If elevation differentials are present, gravity can replace a pressure water system. Taking the conservation ethic even farther, small solar units are available that operate pumps designed for direct current and are capable of pumping a small but continuous stream of water from wells during bright sunlight hours. Adequate storage to accommodate usage during prolonged cloudy conditions, or an electrical backup system, will make such an energy-saving installation viable.

Much frustration and expense can be avoided if water systems in cold climates are designed to operate at temperatures below the most severe that are anticipated. The three areas of exposure are at the well head or other source, piping to the residence, and within the residence. If you are inspecting an existing system, make sure that the well head is protected from low temperatures. Many installations include a pressure tank of fifty to one hundred gallons at the well head, using a small structure, or well house, to protect it from the weather. It is important that such structures be adequately insulated, with some source of heat during particularly cold snaps. Remember, insulation does not produce heat; it merely slows the loss of heat.

Depth of underground piping is important in cold climates. Plumbers and pump installers can provide sound local knowledge for their region. Generally, climates that have snow cover during the winter months are less likely to freeze the earth as deeply as regions where insulating snow does not build up, even if temperatures reach similar lows.

Plumbing inside the residence is less likely to freeze when certain steps have been taken. Make sure that pipes inside walls are on the inside portion of the wall, with the insulation between the pipes and the outside wall. This will allow inside heat to protect the pipes from freezing, while slowing the loss of that heat to the outside air. In crawl spaces, exposed pipes can be insulated to delay freezing effects. Perhaps more effective is to block crawl space ventilation during extreme cold periods, allowing ground heat to accumulate. Insulation of any short walls between foundation and floor level also helps. Local building codes may require certain measures to assure water supply during cold weather, but often codes are remiss in this detail. Local conditions may vary greatly in areas separated by short distances or slight elevation differences.

Nothing is quite as valuable as advice from knowledgeable people who live in the countryside close to the spot you are considering. If information about the adequacy of water systems in

Well Water System

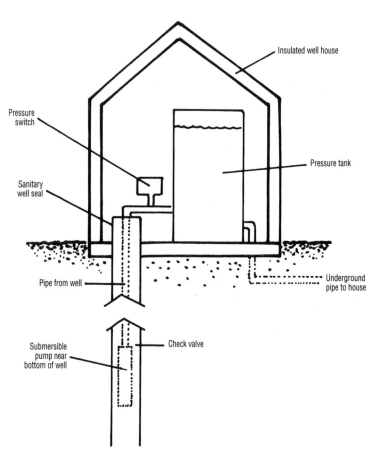

Pressure switch

Insulated well house

Sanitary well seal

Pressure tank

Pipe from well

Underground pipe to house

Submersible pump near bottom of well

Check valve

A common country water system, where a submersible pump is used to pump water into a pressure tank, compressing air in the tank. This compressed air provides continuous pressure, which decreases as water is used. The pressure switch turns the pump on when pressure reaches a preset low point, and off when maximum pressure is reached.

an existing home is desired, it is best to inquire of a local plumber or other professional who has no interest in any particular installation. Neighbors, well meaning but not always aware of the exact conditions or circumstances of adjoining properties, can be misleading in their enthusiasm to be helpful.

WHO OWNS THE WATER?

As areas of our comparatively young nation grew in population, water became an extremely important issue. Areas of scarce supply, such as many regions of the West, experienced "water wars" as powerful livestock ranchers and landowners sought to guarantee their water sources. From these and similar beginnings, water laws have been enacted in nearly all areas, and these laws differ widely.

Particularly in the East, where water abounds, the general philosophy was that whoever lived there owned the water. From this concept, *riparian rights,* the right of an individual to use water that was on her or his own land or adjoined that land, developed. In some areas, riparian rights are taken for granted, because water is plentiful, and conflicts over the use of that water seldom arise.

That is not true in all sections of the country, however. In other regions, all the water in a stream may be owned and controlled for the benefit of a single large portion of land in the vicinity. When such a benefit accrues to a particular parcel of land, that land is said to include *water rights.* Particularly in the West, rights to the water from any source were historically secured on a first-come, first-served basis. This practice led to many a bloody water war, usually brought on when homesteaders fenced water sources, making them unavailable to ranchers to water their livestock.

The first-come, first-served philosophy of *prior appropriation* is still the basis for many water laws in the western part of the nation, as far east as the western slope of the Rocky Mountains. Different kinds of rights to water for different uses are in existence, such as water rights for irrigation or water rights for domestic (household) use.

Irrigation districts, sometimes private but often working with the federal Bureau of Reclamation or other entity, may supply irrigation water for commercial agriculture purposes. Such districts may have vast distribution systems in existence, through canals, ditches, and pipes. Fees are charged for water from most irrigation districts. These fees are often structured so that once land is placed under assessment for irrigation water, the water fee must be paid whether water is used or not.

Unless you plan to use large quantities of irrigation water on your country property, water rights may not be extremely critical. Domestic water, such as is procured from wells, is often exempted from controls, or a different standard is applied that recognizes the comparatively small amount of water consumed by single-family domestic usage. Surface water that runs off your land onto land belonging to someone else is very likely controlled under water rights laws. It is important to know if you can make use of water that may be present.

One way to learn about water ownership in the country area you are investigating is ask the watermaster or other individual representing the state, who is usually located in the county seat. Watermasters are charged with overseeing water usage and seeing that state laws are observed. They are the local water authorities and the best source of information. A local attorney experienced in real estate matters would be another source of information regarding water rights, and real estate licensees may have some knowledge in this field.

Water Problems

Although you as an individual should have few problems in assuring a safe, adequate supply of domestic water in the country, our lifestyle as a nation, aggravated by population increases, now seriously threatens the water supplies across the country. Most evident are the ongoing conflicts involving water in the West. You can be sure that the water wars are far from over, only now the weapons are lobbyists and the courts instead of six-shooters.

Consider the Los Angeles area and its terrific thirst for water. Then think about Mono Lake on the eastern Sierra slope, a lake that has shrunk down to record low levels as a huge pipe-and-canal system drains its life away to southern California. And think about the peripheral canal system in California's central valley, a plan to remove vast quantities of water from the Sacramento River to water populations in the Los Angeles area. Already, in attempts to continue production of agribusiness while sustaining cities, underground water in California has been drawn down to such a degree that in the San Joaquin Valley, some lands have sunk dozens of feet as the water was removed.

Nor is the problem of underground aquifer depletion limited to California. Wisconsin, Virginia, Delaware, and New Jersey have all suffered drought-related problems within the past decade. Arizona, New Mexico, Texas, and Florida are experiencing adverse effects from excessive pumping of underground supplies. The huge Ogalala Aquifer, more than seven hundred miles long and lying northeast-southwest, is showing signs of serious depletion from Nebraska to Texas. No one knows for sure what all the effects of this heavy usage will be, but they won't be good.

And in the true spirit of the Old West, water wars continue over the flow from the Colorado River. All states through which this river flow make claims, the total of which exceeds the amount of water in the river. Even though U.S. Supreme Court justices settled a squabble between Arizona and California in the recent past, the controversy goes on.

Encouragingly, water conservation by the entire populace would result in a surplus from present supplies. It is many times easier, and less expensive, to use less water than it is to obtain more water to use. Very simple conservation methods, inexpensive and requiring no major changes in lifestyle, could bring about this surplus.

One simple change could save our nation hundreds of millions of dollars annually and at the same time reduce the total indoor household use of water by 30 percent. Since the standard flush toilet is the greatest user of water in most homes, reducing the amount of water flushed down the toilet can result in tremendous savings both in water and in sewage disposal costs. Efficient toilets exist today and have been installed in some homes. These appliances use approximately half of the standard four to five gallons required by previous models. A companion saving design to low-flow toilets are dual-flush models, which use a very small amount of water to carry away urine. Is it responsible to continue to use five gallons of water to flush away a cup or so of urine? As you design the water system for your country dream home, keep this particular form of good stewardship in mind.

6

Sanitation

If you live in the country, you will probably be responsible for disposing of your own sewage. In so doing, you will be contributing your share toward responsible stewardship of the natural environment, because subsurface, single-family sewage disposal systems are very efficient at recycling waste, far more so than large municipal systems, which pour billions of gallons of nutrient-rich effluent into streams, rivers, and oceans each day. Besides returning nutrients to the soil, subsurface rural systems cost far less than a share in a huge sewage system.

If your new country home is located in an area where more advanced, ecologically aware philosophies are recognized in the present sanitation ordinances, you may be fortunate enough to be allowed to separate gray water from black water. Gray water is wastewater from showers, bathtubs, and sinks, and black water is that discharged by toilet flushing. Different treatment of these two types of waste are indicated and would result in less water usage, because gray water can be easily recycled for many uses, and blackwater treatment can be more easily accomplished when total water volumes are less. More about this later.

Municipalities routinely provide sewage disposal services to their residents via various types of systems. Sometimes private developments of small country acreages form utility districts and build small sewage plants sufficient for their residents. More than likely, though, when you live in the country, you will be responsible for your own disposal system.

If you buy an existing home in the country, a sewage system will already have been installed. The age of that system, and its adequacy, may be difficult to determine unless it is relatively new and records are available of installation permits and inspections. Even such records may not reveal the entire picture. If you want to be thorough, inspection by a local health department or Department of Environmental Quality sanitarian may disclose whether problems are present. This inspection will only reveal how the system has worked in handling the load of the present occupants, however. Your lifestyle and many other factors may result in a greater or lesser wastewater load.

Ole Anderson purchased a very remote acreage through my office, a piece of land that was mainly deciduous woods, upon which a primitive cabin was located. Ole seemed very much at home in the cabin, and made no efforts to upgrade the sewage system, which consisted of a small, square outhouse about one hundred feet from the cabin. Water from the kitchen sink and an old cast-iron tub went into a small dry well, which occasionally overflowed and ran a few feet down the hillside on the surface.

The county sanitarian discovered the cabin after a few years and was unhappy with the systems. Ole was eventually forced to upgrade the dry well with lateral percolation trenches to alleviate the surfacing of gray water. But because the outhouse dated from a time when such conveniences were allowable, and in fact then the only practical method of sewage disposal, it was "grandfathered" and allowed to remain. Ole was quite happy with his victory. Many present-day engineers and biologists would be pleased as well, for a privy that is well placed away from groundwater and protected from flies is not unsanitary and is one of the least polluting methods of sewage disposal. This is not to suggest that you use an outhouse for your country home, even if you were allowed to do so.

Generally, sewage disposal is regulated by local health departments, local or state departments of environmental quality, or similar organizations. A permit is required before installation, and procedures are set up to determine the suitability of soil types for single-family residential systems. Existing systems are subject to regulation if a failing system comes to the attention of the agency with jurisdiction, or if a licensed septic contractor is called in to perform a repair.

Single-family systems are generally of the subsurface type. Sewage as black-water and gray-water waste from the residence is collected into a septic tank, where bacteria break down solids. These settle to the bottom, leaving the tank filled with clear liquid. This liquid, called effluent, is piped into an underground leach line, where it percolates into the soil. Some of the water also reaches the surface slowly, where it evaporates. Some water is drawn up into plants, from which the water transpires into the atmosphere. Remember Erma Bombeck's book *The Grass is Always Greener over the Septic Tank*? There is a good reason for that observation!

Many variations on this basic system exist and are in common use in certain areas. Local code will clarify what systems are allowable. In every case, there must be a way to dispose of the liquid effluent, and this is where soil types become important. Water percolates through various soil types at varying rates. A sandy soil allows water passage more rapidly than a heavy, packed clay. In soils with high clay content, restrictive or impermeable layers may be found close to the surface. These restrict or prevent the percolation of water in drain field trenches. It is in these marginal soil situations that separation of black water and gray water can be of real benefit. Gray water can be recycled, after some microbial treatment, and used on lawns and landscaping, exactly where nutrients are needed. The septic tank, now treating only black water, does not overload from a large volume of water flowing through before decomposition of solids is complete. If there is a provision in the local ordinance for gray-water separation, by all means take advantage of it.

The rate of percolation determines what type of system is appropriate and how much percolation area is necessary. Another factor is the number of people using the system, something many codes try to determine from the number of bedrooms in the home. Good percolation means that subsurface disposal of effluent is feasible. Percolation that is too rapid can increase the possibility of polluting underground water supplies.

Various means are used to determine percolation rates. Often exploratory excavation is done to expose the soil profile to a depth of several feet. Soil experts or others with training can then determine the percolation characteristics of the soil and judge suitability for subsurface disposal.

Many years ago, when percolation was determined by drilling holes in the soil, filling them with water, and timing the rate at which the water level dropped, I was helping an elderly rancher who wanted to build a second home on his property. The sanitarian and I filled the test holes with water and measured the level. When we returned two hours later to measure the amount the water level had dropped, we were stunned to notice that the level was now *above* where it had been. The rancher, misunderstanding the process and wanting the holes to be accepted, had sneaked back and filled them again just before we returned. Luckily, the percolation was good, and the second test met standards.

Occasionally, soil characteristics will be favorable for the first foot or so of depth, but then a layer of impermeable clay stops percolation. The nature of the soil from the surface down to a depth of three or four feet is generally considered in determining specifications for subsurface systems. Where soil conditions are good near the surface but not suitable at greater depths, systems may still be allowed in many sanitation codes.

One method to counteract shallow soil is to fill the area with sand or a good percolating soil to achieve the required depth. Called cap and fill systems, or similar names, such installations operate well but cost more to install. Other deficiencies in soil can often be corrected by engineering a system to fit site conditions. In almost every case, additional cost is involved over and above that of a standard system.

In evaluating a parcel of land for purchase, it is important to determine the suitability of the site for subsurface sewage disposal. Most codes address many factors in addition to the soil type and resultant percolation ability. The amount of land area involved is considered in determining whether a satisfactory system can be installed. Usually local and state codes require minimum setbacks from property lines, to assure that there is no leaching of effluent onto neighboring property. Often there is a requirement for a replacement or repair area. This allows enough space if the original installation becomes clogged over time because of usage and a new leach field must be installed.

Slope, or gradient, of the land surface is another factor. On land that is too steep, effluent can flow out to the surface instead of percolating into the soil. Codes often limit the slope on which subsurface systems can be installed.

Proximity to water supplies and bodies is also considered. Distance from wells, springs, streams, lakes, ponds, and even seasonal watercourses is strictly regulated to avoid polluting these sources. Codes vary, but distance requirements from water can be one hundred feet or more.

Water bodies can play other roles, though. Some systems utilize small ponds or lagoons, in which bacterial action decomposes sewage. Such installations require construction of the lagoon in a manner that controls percolation so that pollution of groundwater will not occur. Often this means using clay to provide an impermeable bottom to the pond or lagoon. Microbial action reduces sewage solids to a sludge, which settles onto the bottom of the pond. Such systems work best when there is sufficient sewage and wastewater flow to maintain design levels in the lagoon, a requirement that single-family dwellings may be hard pressed to fulfill. Evaporation from surface areas is relied upon to regulate water levels.

It is not unusual in country properties to find situations where the best location for a subsurface leach line is some distance from the site of the home. Such suitable areas can be used for disposal, even if they are uphill from the homesite, by installing a simple collection tank for effluent near the septic tank itself. An automatic system then pumps effluent to the site of the leach lines when the collection tank becomes full. Codes often require that the collection tank have a capacity of two days of use, in case of repair or power failure.

Whatever the type of sewage disposal system in general use in your particular region, standard systems of that specific type will probably be least expensive to install. Contractors are more highly experienced in installations of the standard type. Engineers are often able to overcome site deficiencies by designing special systems to compensate for unusual problems, but many of the special systems that compensate for soil or other site deficiencies involve more material and labor, as well as excavation, and are therefore more costly to install.

There is a subtle but direct relationship between the type of system that can be used and the value of the acreage. The value difference is probably equal to, or somewhat greater than, the cost difference between the two systems. It is important to determine the suitability of a parcel of raw land for subsurface sewage disposal before finalizing a purchase of that land, for two reasons. First, you need to be sure that some sort of system will be allowed. Second, the final negotiation for the land might reflect consideration of just what type of system will be necessary and, if it is a special system, the added cost involved. Sometimes this factor has been already calculated in the sale price of the property.

Some reflection regarding living conveniences is appropriate in this chapter on sanitation, although most involve water usage every bit as much sanitation concerns. Advertising and marketing efforts have created certain expectations on the part of homeowners that are not ecologically sound. Such things as garbage disposals, automatic washers, and dishwashers have great effects on water usage and the ensuing necessity of disposing of the used water afterward.

Garbage disposals are convenient, but these devices require considerable amounts of water to flush ground garbage into the sewer or septic tank. Resultant solids increase the load that microbes must handle to reduce these solids to sludge and liquids. Heavy use of a garbage disposal unit can double the load of solids introduced into the septic tank, as well as greatly increasing the flow of water through the system. Many experts are now recommending that garbage disposals not be used at all, especially in country areas where biodegradable refuse can be easily composted.

Automatic washing machines and dishwashers are certainly convenient, but there is no question that they use a lot of water. Unless gray and black water are separated in the home's plumbing system, these large quantities of water flow into the septic tank and then must be disposed of through the drainfield. Realistically, these appliances are so convenient that their use is unlikely to be diminished, at least until water supplies become much more scarce and treatment and distribution expensive. What the homeowner can do to benefit the environment is to see that these appliances are not operated unless there is a full load being cleansed. Some automatic laundry manufacturers offer "sudsavers," which recycle that portion of the wash water that contains the detergent. These are excellent systems.

The standard flush toilet is the greatest culprit in excessive water usage. It is highly unlikely that the more radical designs, such as composting toilets, will become popular. The problems of water supply and sewage disposal are not perceived by the general population as being serious enough to warrant such drastic measures. What can be done, as recommended in the previous chapter, is to install low-flush toilets, which cut water use by the toilets approximately in half. Existing toilets should be replaced or upgraded with dual-flush valves.

Though some public entities are now practicing conservation through use of low-water-use toilets in public restrooms, most are not. Some of the less exemplary are the very cities in which water shortages are most severe. It is up to the people to bring about the necessary changes. Country dwellers have many opportunities to promote good stewardship, and the very best promotion is by example.

7

Utilities and Other Services

During the early settlement of this country, people got by with very little. Electricity and telephones were not part of residential living. Sewage disposal was via the simplest route, the outhouse serving one function, and kitchen and bath wastewater being simply thrown outside, perhaps on the garden, as it is today in many developing countries. Garbage was made up not of packaging but of portions of food inedible to humans, which was prized as food for animals. Water was rarely piped; delivery inside the home usually required a trip or two with buckets. But water was vital, the one necessity.

Matt had decided to restructure his lifestyle in the simplest manner possible. It made no difference to him that now, at the end of the twentieth century, few deprive themselves of the comforts that have become such an unconscious part of modern living. The forty acres he purchased could be reached only by four-wheel-drive vehicle, and then only in the summer. Matt didn't have a vehicle, but his friend did. He spent several months on his land, meditating and building what could, with kindness, be described as a cabin. The size, design, and workmanship of the structure caused speculation as to just what Matt had been meditating about. Although there were county building codes, the cabin came into being without the blessing of the inspectors.

Matt spent one winter at his cabin before hitchhiking in to my office to list the property for sale in the spring. That he had managed to stay there at all during the winter was a wonder that was more understandable after I visited the site. Somehow, Matt had managed to move in a large, cast-iron wood stove, of such proportions that even a small fire would heat that drafty cabin. Firewood in large quantities had been stacked just outside the door, as bark and other debris indicated. But the biggest surprise, inside the cabin, was an old brass faucet stuck inside a piece of black plastic pipe. Matt had run the pipe all the way from the spring on the hillside above, delivering by gravity a stream of cold, sweet water.

The young couple who purchased Matt's forty acres did so because of that stream of delicious water. They removed the cabin and used the property for summer recreation. Today a new cabin stands on the site, complete with gravity-flow water from that mountain spring. Matt's successors continue to use their property for recreation. Spending a week or two there once in a while is a real treat. The nearest power lines for supplying electricity are three miles away from the cabin, but they don't mind not having TV, and using lanterns for light. Their cellular phone operates well from the site, so they have communication if they want it. But theirs is a remote spot, without utilities and far from services.

Aside from water, electricity is the most important utility for modern living. If you purchase an existing country home, electricity will nearly always already be installed. If you have a burning desire to build your own home on a nice country acreage, you must consider the availability of electricity to the site.

Though a small number of individuals have placed the beauty and remoteness of a location above the availability of electricity, doing so has always been a trade-off with great cost. One property I once had for sale was just such a place. Through the property flowed a wide, swift flowing stream bordered by aspens and pines, a stream that flowed from a huge spring and varied but little with the seasons. The home and outbuildings beside the stream were somewhat nondescript. What set this place apart was a huge waterwheel set in the middle of that large, beautiful stream.

Generous flows of water turned the wheel and the geared-up electric generator to which it was belted. The result was a modest but continuous amount of electricity and freedom from the electric company. This waterwheel place, thirty miles and an hour and a quarter driving time from town, was also the most remote property we had ever sold for an owner. It was purchased by a couple who lived there with their children and made their living by lecturing and writing books on self-sufficiency.

Most of us demand electricity from usual sources in our homes. Without electricity, there is no forced air, dependent upon electric blowers for air movement; no instant light at the flick of a switch; no small appliances such as toasters, blenders, or hair dryers; no power tools; no TV, computers, or word processors. Any number of everyday conveniences we take for granted are unavailable.

Home heating is possible without using electricity, largely from space-heating stoves burning wood, coal, or other fuel. Efficient refrigerators that use liquified petroleum gases (LPG) such as propane or butane are available. Lighting and cooking with appliances using LPG is feasible, as is heating water. With some inconvenience, these basic necessities can be provided without electricity.

In the same manner as at the waterwheel place, other hardy individuals have installed various alternative systems in order to generate their own electricity. Most common is the installation of a generator. Many institutions, as well as the military, maintain their own generating plants. But institutions have large budgets, able to purchase and maintain quality diesel generating plants to use in the event of a power outage.

Electricity from a generator will usually operate sensitive equipment, like computers, acceptably. Generators fueled by gasoline are most common. Diesel power is more expensive to purchase but less expensive to operate. Some generators will operate using LPG. Because of efficiency losses and motor starting loads, a generator intended to provide two horsepower electrically needs to be powered by at least a four- to six-horsepower engine.

Because we tend to use electricity intermittently throughout the day, generators need to run nearly continuously to provide the convenience we are accustomed to. The size of the generator necessary must be determined by adding up all of the electrical loads that might be operated at the same time, plus allowances for motor starting loads. For an all-electric home, this would mean a very large generator. If you cook and heat water, as well as the home, with LPG, the loads become more reasonable.

Other alternative systems are water, wind, or solar powered. Private water-powered systems are common in areas where dependable, unvarying water flows are present. An ideal situation would be a large spring that flows and drops at least two hundred feet in elevation on the property. These conditions would allow installation of a Pelton wheel, actually a small water-powered turbine, connected directly to a generator. A moderate-volume, high-pressure flow can handily supply all the electricity for a home except that necessary for heating functions. An engineer experienced in hydroelectric power is the best source of counsel in evaluating a site. Water-rights laws, as well as a possible permit system, also will affect feasibility of any water-powered system. Seasonal water fluctuation, such as that caused by storm or snow-melt flooding, debris in the water, or drought, greatly complicates small hydro power generation, as do freezing temperatures.

Wind power is largely unregulated at this time. Unlike water power, which is relatively continuous, wind generation is intermittent, taking place only when the wind is blowing. Storage of the electricity generated, for later use or for intermittent heavy use, is accomplished by using batteries. While battery technology improvements are being made from time to time, it is still very expensive to store large quantities of electricity. If the wind blows steadily at the site, thereby making battery storage minimal, you may wish to question whether you want to live there in the first place.

Solar power generation, using photovoltaic cells, is becoming feasible, although it is still very costly. Here, too, storage of electricity is required so that it can be used when the sun is not shining or during short periods of heavy use.

Other innovative systems for supplying electricity exist and are used largely because the individual enjoys being independent and doesn't mind either the cost or the inconvenience. Most of us, however, will benefit from being supplied electricity by the local power company.

ELECTRICAL SERVICE

Due in no small part to the Rural Electrification Administration (REA), electric lines now run into many rural areas where the customer load was formerly not considered great enough to justify a distribution system. This agency pioneered systems of distribution using voltages suitable for being conducted over long distances on two wires only, thereby lowering the cost. These are single-phase lines, supplying the type of electrical power most commonly used in residences. Single-phase electricity may not be the most economical for operating large-horsepower motors, such as those often used in pumping water for irrigation, but it is all that is needed for domestic, household use.

All residential services, and some electrical distribution system extensions, can be placed underground. Although doing so costs slightly more in most cases, the visual rewards are great. There are few beautiful country locations that are improved by the installation of tall power poles and transformers.

If you are building a home on a country acreage, securing electrical power may require nothing more than dropping a service wire to the new home from an existing line that goes along the road in front. If the site is some distance from an existing electric line, a line extension is necessary in order to provide service.

Line extensions incur costs, which are handled in various ways. Many power companies allow a certain "free distance" when a new service is connected to their system. This distance is calculated based on the amount of investment the power company can justify for the anticipated revenue. Typically, a new home that is electrically heated and thereby will use large quantities of electricity will qualify for a longer free distance than a home that uses electricity only for lighting and cooking. The customer may be asked to pay a certain amount, or all, of the cost of extending the line to provide service. Often a pro rata refund to the customer is made if additional customers connect to the new line within a specified time.

In every case, the policies of the power company regarding new customer connection have been reviewed and approved by the public utility commission having jurisdiction in the area. Companies may interpret some flexibility in their policies.

Power companies usually have right-of-way agreements with cities and counties whereby power distribution lines can be run beside and parallel to roads of these entities. In that way, the power company is able to extend distribution lines to serve new customers without the necessity of negotiating for new rights-of-way for that line. In some cases, the shortest and thereby the least expensive extension is via a direct route that crosses property owned by someone else. If an easement for the power line can be negotiated in these cases, costs are lowered. Often there is a benefit for the property owner who grants the easement, such as having electricity available closer to areas where it is needed, like a barn or well. Power companies may offer the service of negotiating such easements, or this may be left for the customer needing the new service. Placing a line extension, as well as a service line, underground may be less objectionable for right-of-way areas where visual considerations exist.

TELEPHONE SERVICE

Since the proliferation of cellular phone service companies, telephone communication is now possible and practical from locations not served by telephone wires. Commercial communication companies that serve private business with radio telephone service also make communication possible where no wires exist. These, the former a new development and the latter a service that has been around for decades, make conventional telephone service less a concern than it once was. Still, conventional, hardwired service is desirable and may also mean the availability of cable TV in the future, as well as other electronic services and conveniences.

Many telephone companies have reciprocal right-of-way agreements with power companies to run telephone wires along the electricity rights-of-way. The same poles often are employed for both electricity and telephone service. More and more telephone lines are being placed underground, creating less visual impact and requiring less maintenance.

Telephone companies are regulated and have policies relating to installation of new services. Question the local company if you are considering telephone service to a new rural site.

Most small towns are now served by cable TV companies. In some areas, these companies have installed distribution systems some distance out into rural areas. Contact the local company to determine if service is available should you wish to subscribe.

RURAL POSTAL SERVICE

Most country areas are served by the postal service. That rural free delivery (RFD) is widespread is attested to by the millions of mailboxes that line country roadsides. Even so, there are lots of areas farther out in the country where population is so light that no mail service has been established. In some instances, remote mail patrons maintain post office boxes. This means a trip to the post office in order to obtain your mail.

Another common situation is for a number of mailboxes to be grouped together in one location at the end of a rural mail route. These boxes belong to rural patrons located beyond the end of the established route and are serviced by the rural mail carrier.

LAW ENFORCEMENT

Small towns often have their own police force. Even if only one officer constitutes the force, some sort of funding is involved, and for this reason, law enforcement is usually limited to within the town supporting the force, except in emergencies. This means that law enforcement in the country is often provided by a sheriff who serves and is supported by an entire county. Deputies periodically patrol the county area and provide emergency response.

State police, who may patrol roadways in the country, are another source of law enforcement. Such patrols, as well as those by the sheriff's office, may be few, depending on the geographical size of the area and the number of inhabitants.

In the country, then, law enforcement personnel are covering large areas and are available much less frequently. Many forces are able to respond on an emergency basis only. Response time is often long, varying with the driving time to the location. On the positive side, the need for law enforcement is infrequent in the sparsely populated country areas.

GARBAGE SERVICE

Garbage pickup service may be available on a weekly, semiweekly, or monthly basis. Usually the sanitation company serving a nearby town will run a pickup route out into country areas to individual homes. In areas of light population, companies will sometimes provide a dumpster at a convenient country location, into which several or many residents dispose of their household garbage. Billing is then split among those subscribing to the service.

In other areas, no garbage service is available. In that case you must take your own garbage to the nearest sanitary refuse disposal site, or dump. Perform this disposal task a time or two, and you begin to appreciate garbage service. One benefit, however, is that you gain a real awareness of our national solid waste disposal problem. Country areas have not lagged behind more urban areas in environmental programs such as recycling. In most regions there is a high awareness of the solid waste problem, resulting in centers for recycling glass, aluminum, plastics, cardboard, and often other materials. Many small towns encourage such efforts, even though transportation to markets may be expensive.

Recently, in the wake of solid waste disposal regulations, new rate structures have been established that include a trust account to assure proper closing of the dump site when disposal there is complete. In some instances, fully half of the current rate is applied toward eventual costs of closing the dump site. The scenario is unlikely to improve; disposing of garbage is going to be expensive whether you live in the city or the country.

NEWSPAPERS
Local newspapers are delivered to homes by carriers if the country population is dense enough to support a route. In some instances, local papers are delivered by the postal service. Large daily papers from cities may be distributed over routes if the number of subscribers warrants. You also may subscribe to them by mail. Country residents do not live in a newspaper void but may receive some publications a day or two after the published date.

8

Land Selection and Home Siting

Selection of land differs from selecting a geographic area, which involves climatic, demographic, and service proximity decisions. Once you have decided on a geographic area, the next step is to select the land, either an unimproved parcel or a site already improved with a home. It is important that the land you select contributes toward fulfilling your objectives in moving to the country.

It is not the purpose of this book to explore the ideal size for a residence or to influence architectural design. Whether you build or buy an existing home in the country, decisions about your home will need to be made. Where that home will be located within your chosen area is the focus of this chapter. Whether that home is sited on a building lot in town or on a large acreage some distance out in the country, you will be choosing that parcel of land right along with the home.

For a land parcel to fulfill your purposes in moving to the country, those purposes need to be kept in mind during the selection process. If you want to dabble in farming, with some crops or a few animals, good soil and irrigation water are necessary, and you probably need several acres. A two-acre wooded hillside would not be suitable. On the other hand, if just being in the country to relax and live a slower lifestyle is your desire, that wooded hillside may be ideal.

Many young families opt for a small acreage where a few farm animals can be raised. Such a parcel supports the efforts of young children in caring for animals and facilitates involvement in such country organizations as 4-H clubs and Future Farmers. The positive influence of these organizations during the formative years of young people is well recognized, regardless of what vocation lies ahead.

Land value levels vary dramatically in different geographic areas and are sometimes markedly different in microdivisions within the same area that are just a few miles distant from one another. Available investment will determine what you have the ability to purchase, but here are some general rules of thumb regarding value levels within a given area:

1. The value of identical parcels should decrease as distance from town and services increases. This is in compensation for additional time and expense of getting to services.

2. The size of a parcel in the country may affect value. The larger the acreage, the less the cost per acre.

3. The capability of the land affects value. If a single parcel of land is suitable for agriculture, offers a good homesite, and could be used for several purposes, that parcel may have a higher value than a parcel of similar size and location with only a single practical use.

4. The aesthetics of a parcel affect value. If a small acreage offers only a humdrum site for a home, that parcel will have less value than a parcel of similar size and location where the homesite has a view, fronts on a pond, and is adjacent to a grove of pine trees. A parcel that is partially wooded and partially open ground may have a higher value than one that is entirely wooded or open.

5. Ease of development and use affects value. A mildly sloping parcel where all the land can be utilized and that is near existing electrical service has a higher value than a parcel of similar size and location that slopes more steeply and is a long distance from electricity.

6. Aspect, or exposure of sloping land, may affect value. In cold climates, parcels with warm southern exposure may be more desirable and hence have a higher value. In warm climates, cool northern exposures may be valued more highly.

7. Cost of development affects value. If land characteristics require deeper wells and more expensive sewage systems than average, the value of that land may be below average by the same amount or more.

Phil and Karen were insistent as we talked about their real estate needs in my office. They were from a large city and dreamed of moving out into the country. The one part of their dream that they could articulate with certainty was that the acreage they would buy must be at least forty acres. The other physical features they desired in their acreage were pretty much standard for an area like the one we were in: trees, a meadow, a view, a live stream or creek, and a reasonable distance from town.

Driving out into the country with them, on impulse I turned down a side road to an acreage that was on the market. The property was completely fenced, including a wooded knoll at the upper end. From where we were parked beside the creek, we could see all of the meadow as well as the boundary fences. This parcel had the features Phil and Karen had outlined, and if their increasing excitement was any indication, they realized it. The sheer beauty and perfection of that country acreage captured Phil and Karen on the spot.

There was only one problem; I decided to tackle it head-on.

"How many acres do you think are inside the fence?" I asked.

The far boundary was visible through the trees nearly a quarter of a mile away. Phil looked uncertain.

"It must be at least forty acres," he said finally.

I smiled. I asked Phil and Karen if this property was big enough for what they had in mind and was enthusiastically assured that it was. After all, inside that fence was a land parcel wider than the length of a football field and a full quarter of a mile long. Inside that fence was exactly ten acres. It is not unusual for the uninitiated to have little concept of the size of forty, or even ten, acres.

The vision Phil and Karen held was one of privacy as well as beauty. They had insisted when we first talked that they wanted no close neighbors. The land adjoining the end of this acreage was government land and would not be inhabited. They also wanted a view; the elevated wooded knoll provided this. Just as important, there was no possibility of trees located on an adjoining property growing taller and blocking their view. Many people, in the city as well as the country, have regrettably faced this situation. Phil and Karen became landowners.

Level land parcels usually have the widest range of uses.

Level often means bottomland with richer soils. Level land is more easily irrigated, and being bottomland, it is often located nearer to water sources, such as streams or rivers. Such acreages are suitable for agricultural purposes in addition to homesites. The term *level* is relative, of course, since little land is naturally completely level.

Rolling, gently sloping to steep land is harder to irrigate, generally has poorer soils, and may be located far from irrigation water sources. Such land may naturally produce forage for grazing, which may be seasonal or not depending on climate and rainfall. Sloping parcels offer elevation above lower land, and this elevation often provides very thrilling views. Elevation may also mean partial freedom from any fog that forms in valley bottoms, as well as some relief from air-quality problems, which exist almost everywhere to one extent or another. Land parcels, both level and sloping, may or may not be wooded. The term *wooded* describes different conditions in various areas, although trees are always involved. Tree species vary and may be evergreen, deciduous, or a mixture of the two. Usually a property referred to as wooded is covered with a continuous, or nearly continuous, stand of mature trees. It is relatively easy to make cleared land out of wooded land. It is in trying to reestablish wooded land that disappointments occur. Long periods of time, often a lifetime or more, may be required before a forest becomes mature.

Acreages are also classified by whether the land has water frontage. A stream, creek, or river may run through or form a boundary, or the land may front on a pond, lake, or even the ocean. Larger acreages may contain lakes within the property boundaries, and ponds can be found even on smaller parcels of a few acres. Waterfront property is almost always in high demand.

The Ideal Homesite

There aren't many ideal homesites, unfortunately, and a site that is ideal for one person may have drawbacks for another. But there are some general guidelines that will help you in your search for a country spot, whether it has already been built upon or whether you are the pioneer who builds on the site. Climates in the United States can be simplified into four basic types, and for each type, there is a corresponding set of recognized desirable site requirements.

Hot, moist climates are found generally in the South and Southeast. Here, shade is important. Select higher elevations, if available. One thousand feet in elevation will lower ambient temperatures about five degrees. Also, higher elevations may benefit more from prevailing breezes. Make sure maximum air movement is available at the site for cooling purposes.

Hot desert climates are most comfortable when sites provide shade, as well as exposure to afternoon and evening air flows. Shade is not always available, however. Consider construction of dense, thick material, such as masonry, to insulate from and absorb heat during the day and radiate it back at night.

In *temperate* climates, the best sites make use of winter sunlight. Shade is helpful in the summer, as is the cooling effect of transpiration from deciduous vegetation and summer breezes. Water surfaces can cool through evaporation, and if properly placed, they can also add reflected radiant heat in the winter.

In *cold* climates, solar heat should be maximized. Some type of buffering against cold winter winds is also desirable, such as topography or evergreen trees or hedges. Low areas, which may be frost pockets where unusually cold air lingers, should be avoided. Construction with thick insulation will be a benefit, and exteriors should be dark in color to absorb solar heat.

EVALUATING A HOMESITE
If you will be purchasing an existing home in the country, the site on the land has already been selected for you. Some of the effects of siting a home can be changed, even though the basics of the site cannot. Siting is important for many reasons and can dramatically affect the quality of living on any parcel. Varying topography within a parcel, such as when one or more ridges, slopes, or depressions are present, allows exciting choices in siting. Somewhere on your parcel of land is a site that, considering your lifestyle and uses, is the best one for you. The following factors should be considered in building-site selection:
- View
- Privacy
- Climate
- Lifestyle
- Building costs
- Trees

- Use of remaining land
- Access
- Mood

View

Views may be had even from sites on completely level acreages. The view will be outward, on the level, until an obstruction such as foothills, mountains, a tree, or a neighbor's barn interrupt it. If adjoining neighbors plant trees along the boundary of your property, they will affect your view as they mature. The size of your parcel will determine the impact to the view—the smaller the parcel, the greater the effect.

Sloping acreages offer elevation, and obstructions to the view below have much less effect. Many sloping sites provide enough elevation that the view is not endangered at the downslope property line. This may not be the case, however, at property lines that are on the same contour line or elevation as the building site.

There are other view considerations in deciding on the site. Many acreages offer a choice of views, for example, of the mountains above or the valley below. And is the short-range view, which may be pastoral and idyllic in nature, preferable over the long-range view, which, while dramatic, may be made hazy by atmospheric conditions? These choices may be highly individual, but they are there to be made.

Another view factor is the compass direction. A view looking to the north generally will be easiest to look at and more clearly seen than one to the south. This is because in the Northern Hemisphere, the angle of the sun frontlights a view looking to the north and backlights views to the south for long periods of time. This has a great effect during the winter months, when the sun angle is much lower in relation to the horizon and the backlighting that renders views to the south indistinct. The effect of looking to the east or west is about equal, to the west being preferable in the morning and to the east in the evening, except for viewing sunrise or sunset.

Privacy

Privacy may or may not be assured in your site selection. Sheer distance provides privacy, as well as immunity from noise pollution. On a wooded acreage, siting a home in the middle of the woods would probably offer the greatest privacy but may be a poor trade-off with other factors. Privacy to many means freedom from visual and audible intrusion. Visual contact with neighbors may be prevented by topography such as knolls or hills, and degrees of privacy may be provided by tree barriers, as in the case of a house surrounded by woods. An acreage large enough that a homesite can be selected in the middle of it, far from any possible intrusion by others, provides the greatest degree of privacy.

The first resident in the country had no privacy concerns. Then a second resident moved nearby, and then a third. In considering privacy, look carefully at what the future might bring as the countryside increases in population. If there is a vacant acreage adjoining your parcel now, give some thought to how it may be developed in the future. Remember that the owner of that parcel has as much right to build on it in the future as you do to build on your parcel now. But when that development does come, you will have already considered it and minimized the impact upon your site. Thorough investigation to determine what is there now, and what is planned, can avoid many disappointments in the future.

Climate

Can climate be controlled? Not outdoors, surely. But the *effect* of climate can certainly be moderated, indoors and out. The easiest, most cost-efficient way of doing this begins with site selection. Generally, sites benefit from solar warmth in the winter and are more enjoyable if heat is minimized in the summer. The building site can be chosen to work toward these goals.

Cold air flows downward, particularly at night, along gullies, swales, and the areas where slopes begin to flatten. These downward flows create cold spots or frost pockets. Areas not reached by sunlight in the winter will be colder than areas that receive some sun. Warm air rises along ridges and, if not carried away by breezes, accumulates, making ridge locations warmer than adjacent areas. West-facing slopes can be unusually hot in the afternoon because of the more direct angle of the sunlight striking them. All of these conditions are among the most common causes of microclimates and can affect surprisingly small areas, while adjoining areas a few yards distant may be quite different in terms of temperature and comfort.

The annual tilting of the earth in relation to the sun creates our seasons. The angle of the sun in relation to the earth's surface decreases during the winter months in the Northern Hemisphere. In other words, the sun is lower in the sky in the winter. The altitude, or angle of the sun above the horizon, is a basic way that navigators can determine latitude. On the winter solstice, around December 21 each year, the sun at high noon reaches its highest point in the sky, some 21 degrees above the horizon at 46 degrees north latitude, the approximate latitude of Portland, Oregon. At 38 degrees north latitude, near San Francisco, California, the elevation of the sun on the shortest day of the year is 29 degrees above the horizon.

You can calculate the angle of the sun above the horizon at noon on the shortest day of the year, December 21, by adding 23 to the latitude at the site and subtracting the result from 90 degrees. The remainder will be the angle of the sun above the horizon in degrees. Don't worry about calculating minutes and seconds of a degree of latitude, as doing so will improve accuracy less than one degree. Latitude can be obtained from USGS topographical and many other maps.

A valley building site north of 45 degrees latitude may turn out to be a very cold spot in the winter if surrounding mountains to the south rise above a 22-degree angle with the horizon. Such a location would receive no sunshine during the middle of the day on the shortest day of the year, as the shadow of the mountains would extend out to shade the site. As winter passes, the sun's elevation in the sky will increase, resulting in short and then increasingly longer periods of sunshine at the site. Similar solar deprivation can arise from stands of evergreen trees, groups of buildings, or any obstruction that rises above the critical angle to block the sunlight from reaching the site.

Altitude angles of various obstructions can be determined by several means. A simple protractor, available at a variety store, can be used on top of a carpenter's level. With the level in level position and the protractor placed flat side down near the end of the level, you can visually sight along the protractor to determine the angle of that line of sight.

Solar viewers are transparent devices that delineate the path of the sun each month. Place the viewer on a level surface at your site, and look from the viewing point through the viewer to deter-

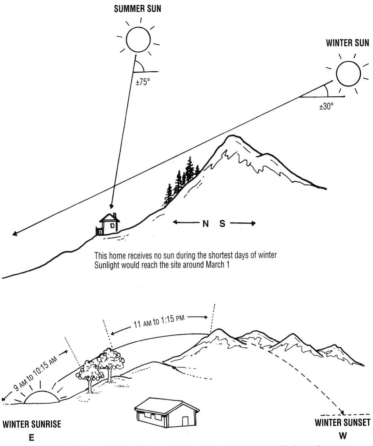

SUMMER SUN

WINTER SUN

±75°

±30°

← N S →

This home receives no sun during the shortest days of winter
Sunlight would reach the site around March 1

11 AM to 1:15 PM

9 AM to 10:15 AM

WINTER SUNRISE
E

WINTER SUNSET
W

Deciduous trees weaken the sun's rays on this home during a 45-minute period in the morning
Nearby high mountains obstruct sunlight completely from early afternoon until sunset

Evaluation of a homesite includes determining solar access.

mine where the sun will be at any given time, any season. Solar
viewers are available from stores specializing in solar supplies.
Simple builder's transit levels can be swiveled upward to read
angles. Another useful instrument is an Abney level, a simple
hand level that can be used to determine vertical angles.

Most sites allow full exposure to sunlight during the summer
when the sun is directly overhead. In all but the coldest climates,
this direct sunlight creates enough heat that it must be consid-

ered. Roof overhang can be calculated so that overhead sunlight will not shine directly through windows until late in the day. You also can determine the direction of air drainage and site the home to benefit from cool, downward-draining nighttime flows. Daytime breezes may exist from predictable directions, allowing siting to take advantage of cooling from the breeze. In very hot climates, reflection of heat and light from nearby surfaces, such as a hillside that faces the site, may be a factor to consider, requiring some sort of barrier to reduce reflected radiant heat. Some barriers, such as deciduous hedges, allow penetration in the winter when it is desirable and prevent excess heating in the summer.

This building site in the hills features excellent views and abundant solar exposure. Most of the trees on this plot of land are deciduous, which will allow a home sited in the trees to receive solar benefits in winter and welcome shade on warm summer days.

Mountain meadows are often ringed by pine trees and other conifers, which provide dense shade during all seasons of the year. Such a feature may be undesirable in colder climates during the winter, although siting a home in a clearing with a southern exposure could maximize the amount of low-angle winter sun hitting the house.

Lifestyle

Choose the site with your lifestyle in mind. A family with young children, for instance, might find that a site on level or gentle topography would be suitable for the outdoor activities of the children, whereas a site on a steep slope would be severely limiting. Lifestyles that revolve around spending a lot of time indoors may be enhanced by sites that bring the home up close to the landscape. Or retirement in the country might mean the desire to enjoy solitude and views without the necessity of maintaining excessive landscaping or grounds. Such a living style can be provided by keeping the site small, selecting a striking view, and using natural features and plants in minimal yard areas.

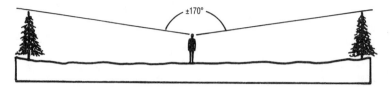

Tall obstacles, such as trees, at the border of a sizable acreage usually do not prevent long-distance views

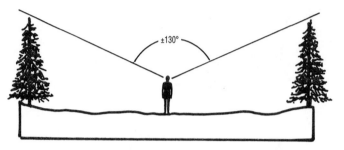

When tall obstacles surround a small site, the viewing angle decreases dramatically; the horizon probably will not be visible

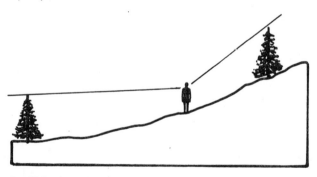

Downhill obstacles on a sloping site usually do not block long-distance views; obstructions that are uphill usually block everything beyond them from view

Giving thought to views, existing and future, pays big dividends. In the winter, bare deciduous trees may allow views that will be completely blocked in summer. Different tree species grow in height at varying rates.

Building Costs

Building costs are definitely affected by site selection. Factors may include distances from existing roadways and to electricity. Sloping sites may require excavation over and above that required on a level location, and they are more likely to involve dealing with hard rock during excavation. Foundations may be more elaborate on hillside locations, and adequate drainage to protect against sudden heavy deluges will be more complicated and expensive.

Trees

Trees, their species, size, and location, have dramatic effect on building sites. Evergreen trees, which have foliage year-round, block the sun and provide continuous shade. Deciduous trees, which lose their foliage in the winter, provide shade in the summer and allow passage of some sunlight in the winter. The difference between the two types can be exploited in site selection to achieve the desired solar control.

The size and location of existing trees affect sites more than is

Five acres of irrigated land can provide a fine homesite and be productive as a small farm. This plot contains a home, a large garden, pasture for livestock, and space for a family orchard. Where summer rainfall is scarce, irrigation is vital to maintaining land used in this way.

usually realized. Many species of trees continue to grow in height, and future view or solar impairment should be evaluated. Evergreens can be used to block undesirable views or assure privacy. Usage and evaluation of existing trees will be most useful, for although plantings can be used to achieve certain effects, the time required to do so may stretch to a decade or more.

Use of Remaining Land

Present and future land usage, both on your ownership and the adjoining, will affect site selection. If you plan on raising a few farm animals, distancing your homesite from the agricultural portion of your property may be advisable. If neighboring owners already carry on an intense agricultural activity, as is common in the country, siting your home so that odor and unsightliness is minimized may be a good idea. Distance, barriers, or both would modify effects in this example. Sound, as well as odor, is more noticeable downwind. Prevailing airflows can be used as buffers in many instances.

Access

Existing roads and traffic patterns affect the privacy and tranquility of a site. A site close to a busy road or highway is impacted heavily by traffic, in the form of noise, exhaust, and visual exposure to activity. A private access road to a site located near the center of a large acreage minimizes this impact. Evaluate the potential, as well as present, traffic on existing roadways. Some private lanes may be deeded as access to many ownerships that are yet to be built upon, and knowing this would allow you to site your home to minimize traffic annoyance as the area develops. Investigate the possible future usage of any existing road or easement that passes through or runs adjacent to your parcel. If such an easement could eventually be used for commercial hauling, for instance, you would want to know about it.

The additional cost of long access roads is another consideration. Maintenance of such roads may be a factor, as is snow removal in some climates. Gravel is often used as driveway surfacing in the country because of cost or other considerations, a practice that may take some getting used to.

Mood

The mood of a site may be hard to define. Almost on a spiritual level, mood can be determined best by spending a lot of time at a proposed site. Using your senses—what you see, hear, smell, and feel at the site—will do much to put you in touch with your reactions to the site. Visit the site in the morning, at midday, and in the evening, or better yet spend a whole day there. If your time frame is not pressing, spend a day there during each season of the year. Look at the views and the vegetation, listen for sounds, sniff the air, and try to judge whether you respond positively to these stimuli. If you are in the process of purchasing a country place, you must make these judgments in a relatively short time.

Absolute perfection of a site is unreasonable to expect. Though some come very close for their owners, those same sites may be glaringly deficient to others. Site evaluation, rather than being a means of finding a perfect place, is a conscious step toward finding a good place and then minimizing the problems while maximizing the benefits.

9

Planning Your Country Home

Much, if not most, of the U.S. population lives in environments that are highly artificial. Apartments and high rises form a world far removed from nature's ecosystems. Concrete, glass, and plastics surround us. The air is conditioned, filtered, forced, and heated, and cooled, all at great energy cost. Much time is spent in transportation conveyances—trains, rapid transit, buses, and automobiles. Driving is often a stressful race against time that pits driver against driver.

Though suburban living is slightly better, it comes at the added cost of more time in transport, not always well offset by the additional space afforded around the average suburban home. Lawns, trees, and shrubs are little bits of the country present in suburbia, but their relaxing effects are all too often lost because living in suburbs has a high cost in terms of time and stress. It is not at all like living in the country.

There is a tendency among new country dwellers to repeat what they had in the city or suburbs. This habit is probably subconscious, but we have all seen evidence of it: a home designed for the city perched on a beautiful site out in the country, looking as out of tune with the landscape as a boat in the desert. It is still a city home, although located in the country, and many benefits of living there are denied the occupants. It makes sense, then, to give consideration to home design, in regard both to the site and to country-style living.

The most appealing environment is one that smells, sounds, feels, and looks good. For most people, the country in general fulfills these requirements. Embodying the sense-pleasing elements into the design of your home further enhances the country living experience. The environment in cities is such that the objectives of city dwelling design are often to shut out that environment, because it doesn't smell, sound, feel, or look good. The city residence itself thus becomes the environment.

Since there is such great variety among country sites, almost any taste in land features can be satisfied. Superior country home design sees to it that the dwelling fits in with the natural elements of the site. Natural materials such as wood and stone blend in with the trees, soil, and rocks of country settings, whereas concrete plaster, or stucco, is often not harmonious. Colors are important considerations; the colors that are found in nature are the colors that blend with nature.

ORIENTATION AND DESIGN

Once you have selected a geographic area and then a specific location within that area, the orientation and design of the home itself will govern how enjoyable actually living on that site, in that area, will be. Orientation is the relation of the home to the points of the compass. Design here refers to the manner in which the home either beneficially uses, or fights with, the energy flow and aesthetics that surround it.

Part of fitting into the natural scene is the utilization of the natural energy flow. Food, water, heat, and light are all parts of this flow in one way or another. Heat and light occur naturally on every site, though in varying amounts. Food and water are present because of solar energy—the photosynthesis of solar energy is the basis of the food chain. Orienting your home to take advantage of natural energy results in a savings in heating and cooling costs and, more important, ultimately provides the type of ambience and interior environment most of us desire from country living.

Orientation to the Sun

Even in the southern latitudes of the United States, sunshine is welcome during winter months. Northern locations with much colder climates benefit even more from proper utilization of solar energy. Solar availability varies greatly with climate and geography. In regions such as New England, cloud cover restricts sunshine many more days of the year than in Colorado, much of the

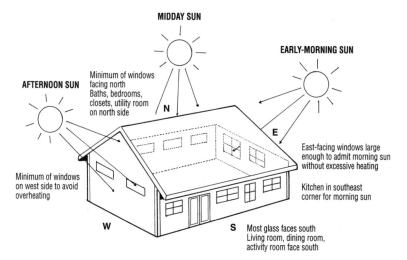

*A well-oriented home benefits from solar energy. Heat gain occurs
mainly in winter through south-facing glass.*

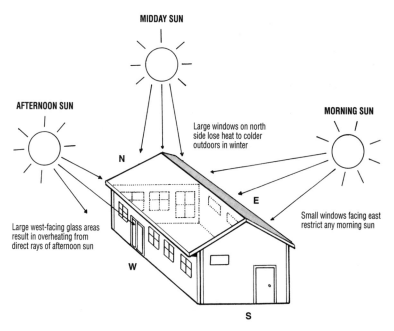

*The poor orientation and design of this home result in overheating in
summer, with little solar benefit during winter months.*

Great Plains, or the Southwest. But even in areas where cloudiness is frequent, there are still many days when sunshine occurs. Many areas with harsh winters have a high incidence of sunshine. Being in, and feeling the effects of, sunlight is an important part of any plan to achieve harmonious living in the country.

Orienting a home to benefit from solar heating also opens the living space to the outdoors, basically through windows. Well-thought-out glass areas contribute more heat than they lose because of their orientation. Glass areas that bring the outside indoors visually do much to harmonize country living with the surroundings. Living in such a home will be bright and cheery, with the advantage of smaller utility bills. Resale value will be enhanced because a future buyer will recognize the value of a home that tends to heat itself in winter and cool itself in summer.

There are two ways of using solar energy in home design: passive and active. Passive solar heating is achieved by admitting sunlight directly into the home itself, producing heat that is controlled in the warm seasons by window placement and shading. Orientation of the home is critical for the best passive solar heat-

Passive Solar Heat

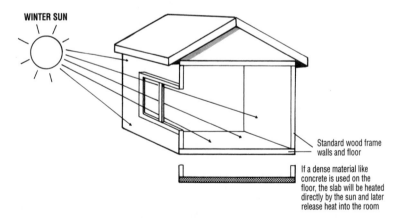

WINTER SUN

Standard wood frame walls and floor

If a dense material like concrete is used on the floor, the slab will be heated directly by the sun and later release heat into the room

Homes designed to benefit from passive solar heating do so without mechanical devices. Movable interior and exterior shading of large glass areas may allow increased heating in winter without overheating during summer.

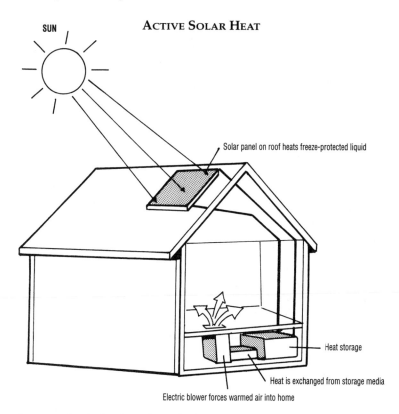

ACTIVE SOLAR HEAT

SUN

Solar panel on roof heats freeze-protected liquid

Heat storage

Heat is exchanged from storage media

Electric blower forces warmed air into home

An example of a basic active solar heating system. Mechanical means are used to circulate liquid through the solar panel and to force warmed air into the home.

ing. Active solar heating uses mechanical devices to gather, store, and distribute the sun's energy. Orientation, though still important, is less critical to active solar systems because the solar collector often can be oriented independently of the home itself. While there are many active solar heating systems in existence, passive systems are more popular because few devices are involved and functioning components are part of the familiar structure. Here are a few specific points to consider in orienting a home to the sun:

• Ideal exposure is due south.

• Exposure within 20 degrees of due south still provides more than 90 percent of available efficiency.

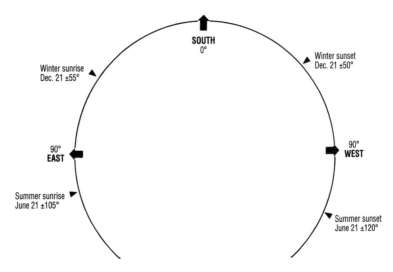

Home orientation guide. *This partial circle locates approximate points on the horizon at which the sun rises and sets at all seasons. Directions are true, not magnetic. Placing a floor plan in the center of the guide and rotating the plan will make it easy to see what the solar exposure effect will be during the day at all times of the year. This guide can be enlarged to accommodate your plan.*

• The longest dimension of the home should be oriented to the south.

• Orienting your home often involves compromises between such factors as view and best southern exposure.

• Small changes in site location can often avoid obstacles to winter sun, such as groves of evergreens or nearby tall mountains.

In reality, your country home will take advantage of only a portion of solar availability. Few sites, and fewer designs, allow perfection in this area, and compromises should be made with other factors to achieve harmonious country living. In all but the mildest of climates, additional heating will be required. What form you use will vary by individual preference and local availability. Most common are electricity, liquefied petroleum gas, fuel oil, coal, and wood. In very mild climates, heat pumps provide both heating and cooling. When ambient temperatures drop below freezing, however, heat pumps may not provide effective heating.

A hillside homesite can reward a builder with fantastic views. The home under construction here enjoys good solar exposure to the south, while conifers provide shade from direct afternoon sun from the west. The builder chose such an orientation on this site to maximize views and provide natural solar benefits.

DESIGNING YOUR COUNTRY HOME

The design of your country home should make the natural environment around you available to the senses. Your home should fit into the site, accomplished through proper selection of natural materials and the architectural lines that define the structure itself. This book will not delve into architectural design, such as geometric shapes and their relationship to each other and their surroundings, but will touch on a few principles that greatly affect country home design if that home is to be in tune with the ecology. There are a few practicing ecological architects out there, but mainly it will be up to the aspiring country dwellers to make sure the features that are important to them are included in any country home, whether planned or existing.

Some important design considerations include the support of a passive solar system and achievement of natural cooling. The home should be suitable for your lifestyle and provide the maximum benefits of country living.

Assuming beneficial site and orientation, the passive solar success of your home can be increased if several design factors are included. First, since *conserving* energy is far more cost effective and easier than tapping it anew, proper insulation is a must. Local and state building codes usually have minimum insulation requirements, but use those as minimum guidelines only. There can be great variations in temperature and exposure within a single geographic area because of elevation and aspect. For this reason, it is wise to insulate more heavily than the codes require. Adequate insulation pays dividends in comfort and in reducing heating costs.

Heat gain or loss occurs in three ways. *Radiant* heat is the major type of heat you feel from sunlight, a roaring fire, or an infared lamp. *Convection* heat is carried by a gas or particles. This is the heat you feel when standing in front of a warm air outlet. *Conduction* heat is conducted within a solid, such as the heat within warm bricks on the back of a fireplace.

Radiant heat transmission is stopped by interception by an opaque solid, such as a wall. Convective heat transmission is minimized by stopping the movement of gas or air, such as is done by insulation. Conduction of heat is slowed by substituting a less dense material or by shielding a dense material with a less dense one.

Insulation is commonly fiberglass batting, or blanket, used in ceiling, in walls, and beneath floors. Insulation does not add heat; it merely slows the passage of heat. Thermal resistance, or effectiveness of insulation, is expressed as the R-value. As a guideline, effective insulation for mild climates would be R30 in the ceiling and R19 in the walls. Local codes and recommendations prevail.

Glass is a great thief of heat when it is cold outside, and it readily allows passage of heat into the home when outside temperatures rise. Double-glazed windows overcome some of these undesirable traits, and triple glazing is even better. Since the architectural impact of windows cannot be overlooked, and large windows function to bring the outdoors in, some trade-off with energy conservation must be considered. Certain types of glass, as well as reflective coatings, can reduce unwanted heat gain from west-facing windows, where sunlight is most intense late in the day in summer. Triple glazing of north-facing windows, as well as employing special glass, will reduce heat loss while still preserving views in that direction. While multiple glazing reduces convection and conduction losses, special glass is available to help minimize radiant heat loss.

When planning a country home, arrange rooms according to their usage, keeping in mind the outdoor views, solar exposure, and ambiance that each direction offers. Place rooms in which the most time is spent, such as kitchens, living and family rooms, dining areas, and dens, to take advantage of solar exposure and view. Put seldom-used rooms against outside walls with little solar benefits, such as to the north. Closets, bathrooms, storage rooms, and utility rooms can be placed in the areas where sunlight is least available and the views perhaps less inspiring.

In cases where views are predominantly to the north, compromises can be made by designing most-used rooms so that the space is open across the width of the home to allow southern exposure at the opposite end of the same room. Shielding large, north-facing windows at night, possibly with drapes, will add to living comfort by reducing radiation of body and inside heat to the colder glass areas.

CLIMATE MODIFICATION

Roof overhangs, or that portion of the roof that extends beyond the exterior walls, can play an important part in passive solar living. The annual tilting of the earth, responsible for our seasons, causes the perceived path of the sun to dip lower in the sky in the winter. This phenomenon can be used to advantage in a simple way: Calculate roof overhangs, especially on the south side and possibly the west side of your home, to a length that will admit the low-angle winter sun and exclude the high-angle, midday sun of summer. Adjust the overhang to achieve a balance between these two objectives. Chapter 8 explains how to calculate the angle of the winter sun above the horizon at midday for various latitudes in the United States.

Decks are inviting because they provide a transition between

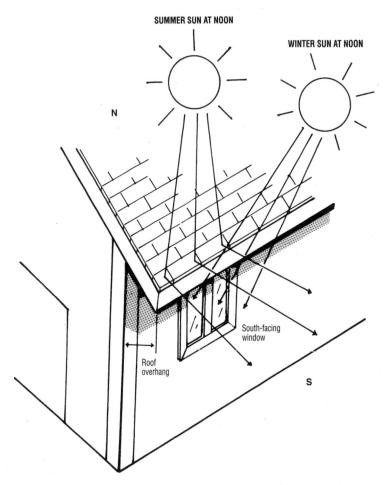

Roof overhangs, especially if oriented south or within 30° of south, can shade a window from midday summer sun and still allow desirable direct sunlight to enter the window in winter.

outdoor and indoor living. Design decks according to season and type of use, taking advantage of solar warmth or more shaded locations as your climate and planned usage indicate.

Exterior colors of the residence affect the way heat is reflected and absorbed. Lighter colors reflect more radiant heat, keeping the home cooler. Accordingly, roofs in warm climates will contribute to keeping the structure cool if they are white, highly reflective, or at least a light color. Color of exterior walls is less critical, because sunlight strikes them at an angle and less radiant heat is absorbed. Still, exterior wall color is a factor worth considering. The heat gain in the afternoon, particularly on west-facing walls, can cause problems that can be solved only with seasonal shading or special design.

In harsh climates, where heating is required for much of the year, dark colors are more advantageous. Heating from solar radiation is greatest on black surfaces. As colors lighten from black to the middle shades, their radiant heat absorption is reduced as more of the solar energy is reflected away. Natural materials such as wood or stone may provide the desired reflectivity for home exteriors and help with temperature control while blending well with the environment.

Ponds, which have highly reflective surfaces, can be strategically placed to reflect solar radiation in the winter. In the sum-

A dense grove of firs overhangs the south side of this mountain home, providing dense shade during the summer. In winter, however, solar access is completely blocked for many hours each day.

Spring buds adorn the oaks and other deciduous trees surrounding this well-sited country home; its location provides dense shade in summer and ample solar access during the colder months. Natural wood siding and a wood shake roof work together to help the house blend well with its environment.

mer, evaporative cooling from the same water body can often be used effectively.

Although site selection may provide benefits from existing trees, often these trees are not of the right species or in the right spot. Deciduous trees provide shade in the summer and allow passage of sunlight through their bare branches during the winter. Local advice and availability dictate what species are appropriate. Planting larger specimen trees can provide immediate benefits, because they are tall and broad enough to provide at least some shade. Trees with a trunk caliper, or diameter, of two to three inches are available, although they are more expensive than the typical wispy plantings. Where a shade tree or trees are an important part of climate control, their cost should be included in the construction budget.

Strong prevailing winds should have been considered in the site selection process, but design modification can reduce their effect. Strong, prolonged winds can be reduced by berming earth close to the home. In extreme cases, earth may be mounded against masonry exterior walls, eliminating the effect of the wind on the underground side. Low walls a few feet away from the home, fencing, dense plantings of evergreens, boulders, or combinations of all of these elements may be used to provide protection. Of special consideration is the entrance, which must be oriented away from storms or protected through design to minimize heat loss from and water entry into the home.

In snowy climates, roof slope can be used to either keep the surface relatively free of snow accumulation or intentionally

This wood-sided home fits nicely into its lakeview site; its metal roof resists fire and sheds snow easily.

accumulate an insulating blanket of snow. Steep pitches shed snow best, and metal roofing materials help even more. Good shedding properties allow somewhat less structural strength and enable longer roof spans because snow cannot build up. The loss of insulation from snow on the roof has minimal effect if the residence itself has been properly insulated. Shed snow builds up where it falls, however, and can block entrances and windows. Pay attention to direction of roof slope to avoid snow piles in unwanted locations.

Low-pitch and flat roofs allow snow accumulation. Although this snow blanket provides good insulation, it also creates some hazards. There is no certainty that the total accumulated load will not be greater than anticipated. As a result, very strong structure is required so that the roof does not collapse. Leak potential can also increase as ice builds up and melting occurs, allowing water accumulation at locations and depths that may exceed design capabilities. One advantage to low-pitch roofs in moderate-snow locations is that eave troughs may be used on the roof and will not be torn away by blocks of snow sliding off. Snow also melts from the roof without shedding into large piles on the ground.

Designing for Lifestyle

Your country lifestyle may be extremely active or quite relaxed and not oriented around outdoor activities at all. Whatever your preference, keep your lifestyle in mind when you design your home.

If you will be involved in much outdoor activity, design the rear entrance to your home so that it can accommodate such things as muddy boots, jackets, coats, and some means of cleaning up before entering the balance of the home. "Mud room" is a descriptive term often used to describe such a space, which also often doubles as the utility room and contains laundry facilities.

You also can create storage areas designed specifically for equipment used in outdoor sports and other activities. Such items are sometimes bulky or odd shaped, and you are familiar with your particular requirements. Inside storage is desirable to avoid rodent damage.

Most important in designing for your particular lifestyle is to make sure that the things that attract you to the country, to a par-

ROOM PLANNING OUTLINE

Space	Used by	Used for	Size	Facing	Near or adjacent	Characteristics, atmosphere
kitchen	mother father	cooking, food storage, eating at bar	10 x 12	south, east	living room, dining room	Convenient, efficient, open to dining and living rooms
utility room	all	laundry, cleaning and storing clothes	8 x 10	north	entry	easy to clean, bright, lots of storage
bathroom	all	toilet, bathing	6 x 9	north	hall, bedrooms	bright, outside windows, easy to clean, tub plus shower
bedroom	mother father	sleeping, dressing	16 x 19	north, east	master bath, walk-in closet	invites outdoors in, still private with morning sun
bedroom	children	sleeping, dressing, playing, studying	12 x 14	north, east	hall, bath	built-in desks, storage closet, light, cheery
dining room	all	eating meals (some formal)	11 x 13	south	kitchen, activity room	open to kitchen and activity, view, solar access
activity room	all	gathering, children playing, entertaining	15 x 20	south, or any	living room, dining room	fireplace or wood stove, storage closet, functional
living room	all	entertaining (formal)	19 x 22	south	activity room	view windows, expansive, formal
den or office	mother father	files, computer, records	9 x 10	north	kitchen or any	allow concentration, storage, efficient

ticular spot or site, are not shut out from your day-to-day living experience. If a certain view inspires you, bring this view inside. If the ambience of your spot is pastoral and peaceful, design living spaces that will put you in touch with this peace and allow a relaxed living style in your home. Think of your home as placing you visually *in* the scene that is so attractive. Design and decorate to make your home seem a part of all the elements that attract you.

10

Distance—Good or Bad?

George and Eileen had spent four years discussing and visualizing their dream of moving to the country. During that four years, they both worked and saved the necessary money. They had refined their vision in their minds until it had crystallized.

"We just want to find a small acreage with a creek and a view," George declared when they visited my office.

"And a waterfall," Eileen added. "Don't forget the waterfall."

There were a few small waterfalls in the city park and others on public sites around the county, but waterfalls on privately owned land are rare in Oregon. George was carrying one of my newspaper ads describing 160 acres for sale. On that land was not only a creek, but also a sizable waterfall. The ad was headlined "Remote Shangri-la." George and Eileen insisted that this was the property for them, brushing off my admonishments that the property *was* remote.

After an hour in my car, the last half of it on continually narrowing gravel roads, small talk was waning. Finally the road led up and away from the creek we had been following, crossed a small wooded bench where the gravel became dirt, and ended at the foot of the waterfall on the property. Even with the low water flow of late summer, a slight mist covered the small pool at the bottom of the falls, reflecting rainbow colors.

The waterfall worked its magic on George and Eileen and on me. It is impossible not to be impressed with the beauty of water tumbling over jagged rocks, free falling into a pool below. We walked around on a few acres near the falls, but I could see that their enthusiasm was much reduced. While George and Eileen were thrilled with the waterfall, they were shocked by the remoteness. The time required to reach the property had been devastating for them. I didn't need to point out that electricity was more than four miles distant. George and Eileen didn't buy that waterfall acreage.

They didn't purchase a property with a waterfall or even a creek on it. Convinced that they had found the geographic area in which they wanted to locate, they applied their resilience and common sense to revising their dreams, and within a week they had purchased a small acreage about five miles from town. Their property had a nice view from the homesite, and some wooded land, but most important to them now, it was less than ten minutes from town. The country lifestyle about which they had dreamed for years was available to them on that acreage. There they could realize the best of two worlds.

In many geographic areas, distance from town and services can be equated with natural aesthetics. The farther from town or services, the fewer people live there and the more beautiful and pristine the countryside.

Historically, towns have grown up along transportation routes. Transportation routes, by their nature, tend to be in lowlands or valleys, although a few routes also lead through mountain passes. Travel routes also tended to keep to open land, away from forests where passage is difficult. When all of these factors are taken together, it is easy to see why many towns, particularly in the West, are not located in the middle of the type of country aesthetics many city dwellers covet. These town locations offer convenience, but aesthetics may not have been high on the list when that small town was first formed.

One definition of an aesthetically pleasing country environment would be an area that remains as it has evolved in nature, without substantial change by or impact from humans. The aesthetics exist in and around trees, mountains and hills, desert and plains, clean water and air. Of course, a certain amount of change is considered beneficial. It would be nice if we could drive there in an automobile and turn on a light or use a telephone once we were there. Distance from town can be viewed as a sliding scale along which the aspiring country dweller can select the balance between aesthetics and whatever degree of practicality he or she feels is necessary.

Perhaps because of the wide open spaces found in the western United States, contrasting with the close proximity of population centers in the East, there is often a difference in the way residents from these two general geographic areas perceive distance. In Nevada, a one-hundred-mile drive to services may seem routine to long-time residents, while that same distance and drive might be beyond the perception, or tolerance, of someone from the East, where population and services are much closer together.

Of the many pitfalls facing those moving to the country, determining acceptable distance to town and services is an arena open to serious misjudgment. First, distance is relative. To a person who routinely spent two hours commuting in the city, living in the country as far as twenty miles out of town may be a real treat because it only takes half an hour to get to town. To a long-time resident of a small town who is accustomed to walking everywhere, living five miles out, where one must get into a car to go anywhere, may be perceived as very remote living indeed.

The perceptions of both residents can change gradually with time, once routine is established. Getting into the car and driving for half an hour to get to town for shopping, social activities, or other reasons may become less tolerable to the former city resident with the passage of time. Gradually, the new lifestyle encourages a slower pace, time at home takes on new value and meaning, and there is a desire to shorten the duration of any activity that detracts from the total quality of life. Under these circumstances, a long drive causes resentment. The former small-town resident, accustomed to walking everywhere, may find a new freedom in living a relatively undisturbed life out in the country, while still being only minutes from town.

The aging process can be another factor in distance decisions. In active middle age, for instance, a thirty-minute drive to town may seem insignificant. As years pass, the same drive may become more and more onerous and reach the point of intolerability. Such a drive involves energy expenditure on the part of driver and passengers that may offset some of the benefits of living in the distant location. The solution is usually a relocation nearer or into town for the former country resident as infirmities progress.

A closely related consideration is the distance to medical facilities. Unfortunately, in this context distance means time. Modern medicine has evolved procedures and treatments that in many instances reduce formerly fatal incidents to more or less routine events. A common denominator in successful treatment of such emergencies is time. How much distance, and therefore time, is acceptable is left to individual judgment. The decision of a high-risk individual to locate thirty or forty minutes from medical facilities can be made only by the affected party or parties. In the minds of some, the peaceful lifestyle of the more remote location may mitigate the condition and may lower risk, or it may be so welcome that any risk is offset.

Medical response by emergency medical technicians (EMTs) is the rule today, even in country areas. Most are extremely well trained individuals, who regularly upgrade their skills. For an EMT or doctor to be of assistance in a medical emergency, the patient must reach that assistance. Assuming a one-way trip of patient to assistance or assistance to the patient, the most rapid help possible can be estimated at one and a half minutes per mile of distance. Before hospitalization is possible, double that time may elapse. Poor roads or weather conditions will further increase this response time.

Another distance-related consideration is the response time of fire-fighting units. While most city and town departments do an excellent job of responding to alarms because they are close to the fire, response time increases with distance to the fire. The many excellent volunteer fire departments notwithstanding, a serious fire out in the country will likely lead to complete loss of the structure involved. This is true simply because the time required to reach the fire exceeds the time required for the structure to become fully involved. This is a fact of life among realistic country residents. If you fail to extinguish a structure fire yourself within the first few minutes, don't expect the fire department to save it for you. They will probably arrive in time to prevent the fire from spreading to other buildings.

The distance-cost ratio can be a consideration in selecting the right country area in which to locate. A hypothetical family living ten miles from town, driving a vehicle to town and back an average of two times per day, will incur costs from that drive of around $4,200 per year, including fuel, insurance, depreciation, and maintenance. Halve the distance, and the costs drop to half. Double the distance without reducing the number of trips, and transportation expenditures rise to $8,400 per year.

Conservation of fossil fuel resources is of concern to all. Comparisons here are simple. If a new country resident, fresh from the city, now spends more total time weekly driving a car than was the case previously, the change has resulted in more fuel consumption. Less time driving than before means a savings in fuel. Other energy uses will probably be about the same, whether living in the country or in the city. Heating with that renewable energy source, wood, is common in country areas. Where population is light, air-quality degradation from wood smoke is minimal.

One fact of country living is that nearly all trips to services will be in the same direction and destinations will be closely grouped in the same area. Normally, schools, shopping, and employment in town are located within reasonable proximity to that town. This is quite different from many city environments, where schools may be in one direction, different stores in various directions, employment yet another direction, and outdoor recreation a great distance away.

As we have seen, distance away from services, as found in country living, is a relative thing. A rancher friend lives about 70 miles from town, and when his two boys attended high school, it was necessary for them to board with friends in town. Two round trips of 140 miles apiece per day was too much, even for those accustomed to wide open spaces in their Great Basin ranching country. I consider their ranch to be remote. Many people mistakenly equate seclusion with remoteness, but seclusion can be obtained without a location being far out or at great distance from services.

One of the more secluded homes I have visited lies only a few miles from town, nestled in the center of a wooded acreage. The topography forms a half bowl, opening out toward forested public land. From the homesite, no other habitations can be seen or heard. Once at the site, you are aware only of the trees, bushes, grasses, and wildlife that surrounds this delightful spot. Jump in the car, though, and in ten minutes you are at the new McDonald's in town, the bank, or the post office.

Seclusion is being off by yourself. Although distance can certainly provide seclusion, other factors can also. Topography and trees very commonly provide seclusion, because they are barriers that separate one site from the next. Such barriers are probably preferable to distance in providing seclusion and privacy, because less time is spent in travel. Distance, however, will often provide seclusion even when barriers are not present.

To decide how far from town is too far, respond as honestly as possible to your own series of questions about the location, which may include the following:

1. Does this location pose unwise medical risk?
2. What will travel cost be in terms of money?
3. Will living here be worth the travel expense?
4. What will travel cost be in terms of time?
5. Will living here be worth the travel time required?
6. Will social life be adversely affected?
7. What other effects will living at this location have?

If children are involved, time spent on school buses may be a factor. Also give thought to your child's contacts with other children outside school. Will there be sufficient contact to reasonably assure normal social development? While this may be hard to determine exactly, in extreme cases where the nearest neighbor is five miles away, there is little question that this isolation will be a factor in the development of children raised there. Whether this is negative or positive is an individual judgment. The isolation of children from other children to play with can be mitigated, but additional transportation and time will be required.

Privacy and seclusion can often be achieved by searching for a location that is within reasonable distance from services and is isolated from adjoining habitations by permanent physical barriers. Topography and forests are barriers only if you own them. If they are not on your acreage, a ridge can be built on by others, and trees can be felled. For this reason, many owners prefer acreages large enough to provide some buffer area around the homesite. The closer to town a country site is located, however, generally the smaller the land parcel. In most cases it is possible to achieve a balance, a site that is reasonable in terms of distance from services while still being aesthetically pleasing and secluded, a site that arouses your enthusiasm and gives you a positive feeling just from being there.

If distance is a strong negative factor, look for the special property features you seek closer to town. When you do find such a site, it will probably have a higher price than others nearby because of desirability. But keep in mind the additional time and travel expenses a site farther from town will incur, even though initial costs are lower.

11

Land Use

Historically, rural land outside cities in most of the United States, aside from that land in public domain, has been virtually free of use controls. A blacksmith shop may have been built at a crossroads a century and a half ago, or a motel and gas station on land that had highway frontage during the 1930s. Stores, light industry, and even intense agriculture such as stockyards, mixed indiscriminately.

As population increased, towns and cities formed at critical areas when populations reached sufficient density. As the different uses grew closer and closer together, and particularly, closer to one or several residences, conflicts arose because of the effects of certain uses on their neighbors.

ZONING

The concept of zoning arose to minimize such conflicts. Zoning confines certain uses to areas set aside for that specific type of use. In perfect zoning theory, a stockyard would not be allowed adjacent to a group of residences. Grouping together similar uses can minimize detrimental effects on adjoining areas.

As time passed, cities found benefits in planning ahead, zoning areas within their limits for specific uses before the need for the space occurred. This allowed for orderly growth and efficient planning of utilities and services.

In the early and middle decades of the twentieth century, few individuals understood the full implications of population expansion, let alone the pressures that would soon be brought to bear on all areas in the United States where living was enjoyable because of good climate or outdoor recreation. Small towns rapidly became midsize, and desirable country areas also grew in population. A movement of population within the United States has increased demand for living space in Florida, California, and the Sun Belt. There is a well-defined secondary population flow away from the Golden State into the Pacific Northwest. Employment factors, as well as a desire for better climates, have drawn population from the Northeast. And longer life spans plus generous retirements have led to hordes of retirees emigrating to the warmer climes of the South and West.

In the last three decades, environmentalism in many forms has also had much effect on land usage. Outspoken proponents have effect in legislative forums and all other regulatory entities. At the same time, an obsession with rights has skewed legal processes to the degree that common sense and our legal system no longer work as they have in the past. Entire generations mature with the notion that they are entitled to control land in rural areas, without effort or contribution on their part. It is common today to hear city dwellers speak of surrounding countryside areas as "our" land. Completely disregarded is the fact that the countryside has been privately owned, resided on, and farmed, taxes paid, and wildlife sustained by families who own and have lived on that land for generations.

In perhaps the ultimate hypocrisy, it is often the new residents in an area who become vehemently antigrowth. They are here, they have their cozy spot, and by golly it's time to stop these outsiders from coming in! It's time to prevent this beautiful spot out in the country from being "spoiled" by any more residents!

It is when zoning is used as an antigrowth measure that the positive effect of the concept becomes negative. In many areas today, that is exactly the intent of some citizen groups, planning boards, commissions, and others. Ordinances and statutes are enacted that have a confiscatory effect upon the land.

For you, the aspiring country resident, the total result is a double-edged sword. Many of the areas you admire when you visit the country are now off-limits to residences. This channels all demand into the areas where residences are allowed, driving up values sometimes to the extreme. So you are going to pay more for your country location than you would were residential prohibitions not in place. There are many areas in the United States where such zoning is not yet enacted, but these may be areas that in some ways are less desirable.

Zoning vast areas of countryside may have an eventual benefit in that present uses might remain the same. It is common, for instance, to zone tree-producing land as forest, not allowing other uses. Though such action effectively prevents these other uses, it does not guarantee that the forest will be tree producing or economically viable. Much land is miszoned, lumped into categories decided from the courthouse instead of from informed inspection, which might indicate that the land is not suitable for a particular zoning at all. Zoning is no guarantee that what is zoned as forest is indeed forest or even looks like forest land. You, living in the country nearby, can simply be assured that you won't have to look at any homes being built on that acreage.

It is necessary to differentiate between residential use and subdividing. Subdividing means creating smaller tracts of land by dividing larger tracts as they exist now. Subdividing by definition creates more land ownerships within the same space, and thereby the potential for more residences within that space. The eventual result of unchecked subdividing is another town. Residential use is the basic property right of residing on your own land, as it now exists, with no dividing involved. It is this right that has been and is being attacked by some. Every time their effort is successful, you will pay even more to reside in the country.

Counties and cities in various states use different nomenclature to describe zones. Each zoning ordinance includes such things as minimum lot size, setbacks, height, and other restrictions for each zoning classification.

For towns and small cities, classifications might include the following:

1. High-density residential (high-rise buildings)
2. Medium-density residential
3. Single-family residential
4. Commercial or office
5. Light industrial
6. Heavy industrial
7. Special purpose, such as open space, park, or watershed

Country or rural classifications might include the following:

1. Rural residential (with various acreage minimums)
2. Open space or reserve
3. Exclusive farm
4. Forest or woodland
5. Special zonings, accommodating endemic uses

In addition, some rural zonings provide for commercial facilities for recreation in very limited areas adjacent to natural features such as water bodies. Tourist facilities in the form of stores and lodging may be allowed at important intersections along highways.

At issue in many areas of the country is the basic right to live on land that you own. Again historically, residential use in itself was viewed as not in conflict with other uses. An owner could live in his boiler factory, located in an industrial zone, if that owner was willing to put up with the noise. Today the freedom to make this choice, in many zones out in country areas, is in great jeopardy or has already been taken away. Where it has, you can no longer choose to endure conflicting uses even if the benefits of the spot far outweigh the disadvantages for you. But of course the boiler factory could not be placed in a residential area, where it would be intolerable.

Problems have occurred when a resident fresh from city life moves into the country. Odor from livestock on an adjoining ranch is objected to by that resident, and litigation follows. No matter that the livestock and the odor were there before the new resident came. Other scenarios exist, such as a new resident on a county road adjoining forest who suddenly decides to try to put a halt to logging on nearby land, or sues because of log truck traffic that existed in the same volume before the resident came. Or the resident who, having just built a home next to an orchard, sues the orchardist because the usual pesticide spraying is being done. Such actions accelerate movements to prevent residences in country areas.

Zoning has grown beyond cities and towns into the country in many parts of the nation. Some zoning ordinances properly allow residences in zones that are primarily set aside for other uses. To minimize reaction to normal practices in those areas, some ordinances require disclaimers and signed releases before residential permits are issued. The effect is to prevent a new resident from moving into the country and then suing the neighbors to cease normal practices, particularly in agriculture, silviculture, and quarrying.

The more desirable a geographic living area is, the more likely that antigrowth sentiments will be strong in that area. It is in such regions that highly restrictive zoning ordinances are more likely, with increased likelihood that the ordinances were designed as an antigrowth tool.

Before contracting to purchase country property, it is of the utmost importance to check into zoning regulations to be sure that you will be able to do what you intend. Do not take the word of any owner or real estate agent. Check with the local planning authority, the same one to which you must apply for a permit to build. If you wish, you can have a local attorney do this for you.

PERMITS

Most counties have building permit systems in place. Local building codes, usually modeled after the National Building Code, must be followed. Additional permits are often required besides the basic building permit. It is likely that a separate permit for electrical installation will be required, often with a different inspector from a separate agency. The same may be true of plumbing. Septic permits are almost universally required, and many counties or states require water well permits before a well can be drilled. Permits are often required for creating access to existing county roads. Such permits not only take into account matters of traffic safety, but often specify the mechanics of installing an approach onto the existing road as well. This makes sure such items as drainage, if culverts are required, and gradients are addressed.

SYSTEMS DEVELOPMENT CHARGES

The cost of upgrading infrastructure as population increases has spawned a relatively new fee system in some areas. Often referred to as a systems development charge, this fee is charged by a city or county for connection to existing systems. In a city, the systems might be city water, sewer, and streets or other services. In the county, it is often charged on the basis of access to county roads.

The reasoning behind systems development charges is simple. New residences increase load on nearly all existing systems. Since these systems are already in place and were paid for by prior residents, the new residents historically were getting a free ride. Other than maintenance fees, new residents benefited from the infrastructure and paid nothing for that benefit until upgrading was required.

With systems development charges, new residents reimburse the city or county entity for a proportional share of the cost of the existing systems. In rural areas, county roadways are reimbursed, as are the capital expenditures of county law enforcement and any other services the county supplies to its residents. In effect, new residents buy in to the systems that will be serving them.

THE ENVIRONMENTAL PROTECTION ACT

Probably few enactments have had as immediate and far-reaching effects on land use as the federal Environmental Protection Act. As an example, consider the effects of environmental lawsuits against the U.S. Forest Service in the Pacific Northwest. At issue was logging on public land, administered principally by the forest service. There are several subspecies of spotted owl, but one, the northern spotted owl, which is widespread throughout old-growth timber environments in the Northwest, ended up on the endangered species list of the U.S. Department of Fish and Wildlife. Because of provisions in the EPA, grounds were found to issue injunctions against logging in so many forests in order not to impact owls that the entire logging economy of the Northwest ground to a near halt.

It is difficult to fault the EPA for regulating activities adverse to an endangered species when that activity is on public lands. By definition public lands are owned by the people, not the forest service, and impact of federal laws involving use of those lands affects the national population equally. The spotted owl controversy, in which the real issue was logging old-growth timber, affected an entire *private* industry, but that industry did not own the forest land.

A real difficulty arises, affecting the rights of the individual, when the EPA enforcement spills over onto private land usage. In Oregon, curtailments were placed on all activity on private land if such land was shown to be used by spotted owls. This could mean that a tree farm owner might not be able to harvest forest products from, or otherwise use, land that was zoned forest, was in forest use, and had real economic forest potential. Because there is no provision for compensation to the private landowner, such regulations amount to a taking of rights without compensation, a constitutional issue.

Some entities have gone further and developed zonings that take into consideration nonendangered, nonthreatened wildlife in various areas. Privately owned lands, if wildlife usage takes place, can be restricted under these ordinances to such a degree that reasonable use, including residing on the land, is impossible, again without compensation. While there is a long-standing precedent whereby real estate ownership rights may be taken from the individual through eminent domain powers for the good of the greater numbers, landowners have been guaranteed compensation for such taking. The EPA provisions, and other ordinances spawned from its success, make no such guarantees.

There are problems also with federally mandated wetland legislation, which can greatly impact usage of private lands. Some states and local entities have wetland legislation of their own. Definitions of wetlands can be extremely broad, and these definitions can be applied to surprisingly small areas. Better definitions and a moderated application of the statute might mitigate the damage to private individuals, as would applying the principle that individuals from whom property or rights are taken for the good of all the people are compensated by all the people.

STEWARDSHIP

An old rancher I knew was the third generation on his land, which had been homesteaded by his grandfather in the mid-1800s. Fifty years before the rancher was born, his grandfather had taken over the land and developed a ranch with his own two hands. The ranch house was modest, extremely so by present standards, and the barns were honestly built. Water from the creeks had been diverted in order to irrigate fields where hay for winter was raised, but most of the acreage was grazing land on which cattle fed during all but the winter months.

Such usage can be gentle to the land provided the number of cattle is not excessive. Visual impact of the ranching uses was evident only in the hayfields, which were green in the summer instead of the golden brown of dry grasses common in areas not irrigated. There were fences, but not a lot of fences. The ranch to this day presents a pastoral environment at the upper end of the life zone where oak savannas and valley grasslands blend into the foothills that introduce timber slopes above.

This rancher believed in stewardship of the land. His approach, like that of his father and grandfather before him, was to preserve his land holdings so that they would continue to produce for the next generation, and the next. He reveled in the presence of wildlife and was profoundly affected by the beauty of nature that surrounded him on the ranch.

A country dweller can damage the land in many ways—for example, by concentrating drainage so that erosion takes place or by removing natural plant cover that has protected fragile soil. Humans can excavate, level, bulldoze, and generally tear up the landscape so that no conceivable number of future centuries will be sufficient to restore that portion of the earth's crust to harmony with natural ecosystems. Humans can pollute water sources, surface and underground, or dump and bury refuse that will remain for a practical eternity. In short, we can really foul up a country place. But this needn't be the case.

The physical capabilities of rural land also can be enhanced to help the land fit into the ecosystem even more effectively than it did before our coming. Wildlife refuges do this, when the activities of humans on the land are geared toward increasing the productivity of that land for diverse species of wildlife. A marginal tree farm, barely supporting coniferous species, can be coaxed into a viable silviculture operation by the efforts of humans over long periods of time. Portions of a dry, rocky hillside can be made virtual oases, absorbing carbon dioxide and releasing oxygen, all the while harnessing the sun through photosynthesis to build humus and soils. Eventually a portion of that dry hillside may offer shade, where, because evaporation is now slowed and more moisture is present, other plants and trees will grow until the whole area is self-sustaining.

Although I advocate strongly the rights of individuals to use their land as they see fit as long as that use does not directly harm others, I advocate just as strongly the responsible stewardship of that land. Others will come after and will need to use the same country land.

Good stewardship means that landowners have a responsibility for the environment. All human activity has impact to the ecosystem; stewardship would require that our activity at least sustain, and not destroy.

Good stewardship means that landowners have a responsibility to their neighbors. Reasonable people can always find reasonable solutions.

Good stewardship means that landowners have a responsibility for and to themselves. Little can provide a meaningful, peaceful life as much as living it in the country surrounded by nature. This is the benefit country dwellers enjoy, whether it comes at great cost or little. You can enjoy it, too.

12

Financing Country Property

The purchase of country property can be very similar to the same process in suburbia, or it can be vastly different. The nature of rural property, which often includes larger land parcels, can make part of the difference. A number of other factors affect the financing of country property.

Value levels in themselves have a lot to do with the ease, difficulty, or manner of financing. Value levels are dependent on a number of factors.

Demand for property establishes final value levels. If there are two or more buyers for every property that comes onto the market, those properties will command a high value. Competition between buyers will cause prospective new owners to overlook defects as well as pricing that is above normal. Competition always exists when demand is high and supply is low.

Readily available employment in an area will affect values of real property there. There will be higher demand in an area where living conditions are excellent and employment is available than in a region with equally good living conditions and no job opportunities.

Accessibility also affects value. If two residential areas offering equally good living conditions are available to buyers employed in a manufacturing area, there will be more demand for homes in the area that is closer to the employment than in the area that is a greater distance away, or even remote. The same principle would apply if both areas were equidistant but one was reached by an unsurfaced road. Similar factors affecting overall desirability also affect value.

Two living regions with identical climate and aesthetics will usually exhibit different value levels if one area is closer to major shopping or service opportunities. Real estate in the area nearest to shopping will usually have a higher value provided all other factors are equal.

To a degree, an established and growing population increases value levels. Once the growth of even a small region has become well established, services are available and the desirability of those services will increase demand for living space. As demand increases, value levels also increase. Where supply of real property is adequate, increasing demand for that property still results in increasing values, only the increase is not as rapid.

Other factors affect values as well. And making a purchase of high-value property is much different than paying too high a price for property. High-value property became so because of demand, and demand is a very good indicator of desirability. A buyer would be paying too high a price for real property if the price is substantially higher than the price for which similar properties in the same area have recently sold.

Often initial investment is at least as important to a purchaser as total price. The major portion of initial investment goes to pay the down payment required to purchase a country property. Those purchasers who have sold a home and are relocating to the country will often have substantial funds available and may be able to pay cash for a country place, eliminating the need for financing. Most of the time, a buyer for country property who can pay cash and does not need financing is in the best position to purchase at the lowest price for which a seller will be willing to sell.

There is a direct relationship between the amount of down payment asked for a property and the selling price. As a general rule, a seller will realize a higher price for real property if the down payment asked is small in relation to the total price. This is because as the required down payment is lowered, more potential buyers will be able to buy. When more buyers are able to purchase any given property, competition for that property increases, and the value level increases proportionally.

Down payments required to purchase country property are

generally higher than the necessary down payment for city or suburban real estate. The major reason for this is that the financing that is taken for granted on city property does not function the same way on many rural properties. If the country property involves a very small amount of land, say an acre or less, financing may be identical to that of city locations. Generally, however, one of the motivations of moving to the country is to have some space around, and this means larger land parcels. By statute or by charter, most banks and savings and loan institutions cannot loan on unimproved land. The parcel on which the home is located can be considered in final value appraisals, but the value of any excess land is either ignored or greatly discounted.

A home located on twenty acres, then, might be considered by a lender as having the same or nearly the same value as a similar home on one acre. You can bet that the seller of the home on twenty acres thinks differently, and so will the purchaser. The resultant spread between appraisals of lenders and actual sales prices of country property has resulted in the practice of owner financing of country property. This usually means that a larger down payment is required than on city property of the same price.

If the country property is a parcel of unimproved land, the down payment required for purchasing that land may be quite small, especially when compared with the down payment necessary to purchase a property of equal value that includes a home. Unimproved land usually provides little or no income to the owner, hence selling it does not involve any loss of income. Selling a property that includes a residence brings about the loss of use of that residence (or the income from it), and this loss must be replaced, hence the common need for immediate offset in the form of down payment to an owner who provides financing.

Other factors determine marketability and, ultimately, value of country property. Middle-of-the-road properties, or those places that have most of the features desired by most people, generally have a higher proportionate value than properties in which only a few individuals would be interested. This higher value is supported by the fact that wide appeal results in increased demand.

To demonstrate the above value-resulting-from-demand relationship, consider the rustic, contemporary home on five acres with a pond that Joe and Madeline purchased. This property was within seven miles of town and very desirable to a wide segment of purchasers. Had the exact same home in the same setting been located forty miles from town on a gravel road, its value would be considerably less. This is because many purchasers would object to the distance and type of road, resulting in far fewer prospects for the property. Fewer prospects means reduced demand, which in turn reduces value.

The demand for property in desirable country areas is high all across the nation. Value levels vary dramatically as features, conditions, climate, and populations vary, but demand exists in every area.

How Sellers Price Real Estate

A few sellers are capable of determining the proper value level when selling their real estate. Such a seller may be experienced in business and familiar with property tax assessment procedures and appraising techniques. Having this knowledge does not guarantee a realistic view, however, especially when the individual is pricing property he or she owns. By definition, all things are especially good when they belong to *us*.

Most sellers, if they are attempting to sell their real property through their own efforts, rely on very unrealistic indicators to establish price. Some sellers actually set a price because they have a need for that exact sum of money. No matter that it is half again more than a similar property recently brought on the market. Other owners, hearing rumors of prices paid for properties in the neighborhood, price theirs at that level or above without verifying these amounts. In many instances, the rumors are false, misrepresenting on the high side. There is a very real, perhaps subconscious, desire to inflate the value of one's real estate.

Many owners also think that buyers go about brandishing large amounts of cash, willing to pay far more than value and making impulsive decisions to purchase. In reality, when searching for a country property, the buyer quickly grasps values in an area simply by inspecting various properties on the market. Unwise purchases are made, but they are the exception rather than the rule.

When an owner is represented by a real estate agent, a different set of dynamics comes into play. The agent does know the correct price range for most properties. But that agent is under pressures that can result in incorrect pricing. The first is that the agent has an intense interest in securing a listing from the owner, because securing that listing means income to the agent when and if the property sells. And when an owner has an inflated value level in mind, the agent often finds it easier to concur with that value level rather than try to persuade the owner to be realistic. One result can be a property on the market, offered by presumed professionals, at a ridiculous price.

A second responsibility borne by real estate agents is the legal and moral need to represent their principal, in most cases the seller. This means that the agent has an obligation to secure for the seller the highest value consistent with the circumstances, and indeed can be held liable if that highest value is not obtained. Often the agent may encourage offering a property above what he or she feels is the correct pricing, in order to secure an offer that is equal to, or slightly above, the perceived value.

It has become commonplace in real estate transactions for the seller to ask a certain price and buyers to make offers at lower prices. This dance is one that functions because of human nature. On occasion, though, when an owner is aware of actual value and correctly prices real estate, buyers who expect to bargain over the price become frustrated over what they perceive as an unwillingness of the seller to negotiate. Such buyers may psychologically rob themselves of procuring a reasonably priced property when the seller remains firm. Look at the appropriateness of the entire transaction rather than being fixated on the offer process.

Common Financing Methods
- Banks and savings and loan institutions
- Other lending institutions
- Government guaranteed programs, through the above lending institutions
- Private investors
- State veterans programs
- Exchanges
- Owner financing

Banks and savings and loan institutions provide a large share of residential real estate financing in the nation. Each has a lending program and rates that are offered by that particular institution at that particular time. Most of these institutions also fund loans that are guaranteed by one of the several government programs.

Occasionally large real estate companies offer financing, but this source is often limited to urban properties. Life insurance companies sometimes finance real estate purchases.

Various federal government programs have been enacted to enable easier financing of real property. The government doesn't actually lend the funds; rather, it guarantees the loan, which is made by one of the lending entities, such as a bank or savings and loan. Some of these programs provide for very low interest rates; others are subsidized to a degree for low-income borrowers. Often certain loan brokers specialize in one or more of these types of loans.

Private investors may be a source of financing on certain properties in country areas. Sometimes such investors advertise in the real estate or loan section of local newspapers. Local attorneys often know of individuals who will provide financing on real estate.

State veterans programs require that the borrower be an eligible veteran from that state, and the property must also be located in that state.

Trades of real estate are seldom possible if we take that to mean that the owner of what you wish to acquire will be willing to trade for what you now have. Fortunately, federal tax laws contain provisions that enable exchanging real property, where in the simplest example, a buyer for your property acquires the property you want, and then uses that new property to pay you for your old real estate. Enlist the aid of a competent real estate agent, a tax accountant, and an attorney experienced in real estate exchanges before venturing into the world of exchanges.

Owner financing may be the most viable way to purchase country property when a substantial portion of the purchase price must be financed over an extended period of time. For owner financing to become a reality, the owner must be both able and willing to provide it.

If an owner is financially able to accomplish the reasons for selling the real property without receiving the entire purchase price in cash at the time of sale, that owner is probably able to finance the purchase. An example of inability on the part of an owner would be when the owner wanted to purchase another property and that purchase required all of the proceeds of the sale. Or some other unavoidable cash need might make it impossible for the owner to finance the property sold.

If a seller is financially able to "carry" the balance, that seller would receive regular payments from the purchaser, together with interest, until the balance was fully paid, in the same manner that a bank or savings and loan would receive payments. The balance owing would be secured by the real property sold. The seller, in effect, would become the bank, and there are several advantages. First, repayment can be tailored to fit the needs of both parties. Second, there are income tax provisions that may be favorable to the seller when down payments are below a certain level and the balance of the purchase price is received over several years. (Consult a qualified tax accountant for details.)

Advantages for the purchaser may include not paying a loan fee and the custom structuring of the repayment schedule. Sometimes a smaller-than-usual down payment may be accepted if a substantial lump sum payment is made within a few months or years. If such a situation fits for the seller and is within the capabilities of the purchaser, this device can enable a sale. Nearly any legal conditions can be agreed upon between buyer and seller and incorporated into the financing terms, something next to impossible to arrange with a lending institution.

Though not possible with most lending institutions, many different arrangements may be made with a seller who provides financing, arrangements that are beneficial to both parties. For instance, a purchaser could agree not to pay more than a predetermined amount on the obligation for a specific number of years, guaranteeing the seller a certain income. If it became necessary to prepay the obligation, a penalty agreed previously would be incurred. Lending institutions regularly do this through prepayment penalties. The difference is that the lending agency is not willing to give up anything for the benefit, whereas a knowledgeable seller may be willing to grant a price reduction or some other benefit. Owner financing can be the most flexible tool around when buying or selling country property.

In some cases, personal property might constitute part of the transaction. Bob and Evelyn came into my office searching for a small retirement home in the country. At the time, they were driving a medium-size motor home that they had purchased in order to tour the entire United States. After two months, they realized that a life of continuous touring was not for them; they wanted to settle down. Among our listings for sale was the Blakleys' place, a newer, modest home about ten miles from town, in which the Blakleys intended to retire. But living in one spot bored them, now that there were no regular jobs to take up their time. As they had put it when they listed the home for sale, "We want to travel!"

It is easy enough for you to guess that the motor home became the down payment on the Blakley place. I don't know whether the Blakleys are still traveling, but the point is, every individual has a dream or desire that is different from everyone else's. When sellers are willing to become involved in financing the property they are selling, there are often real benefits to both parties.

13

Title and Title Insurance

George Izacs telephoned me to ask if I would sell his property, which was ten acres of wooded land that included the very minimal house in which George lived. When I met with him to inspect the property, George couldn't find his property tax bill. I completed the listing agreement, which George signed. The next day, researching at the courthouse, I found that George wasn't listed as the owner of the property at all—two other people were. Back with George again, he recognized one of the individuals as the person from whom he had purchased the property but didn't know the other. He had paid cash, George informed me, and the seller had given him a deed. George did not record the deed and gave no thought to doing anything besides moving into the property. Trust is commendable, but George made some bad mistakes.

It is rare these days to discover a primitive transaction such as the one George had been involved in. Most everyone has some basic understanding that purchasing a piece of real property is more involved than just paying someone the funds. Still, trusting individuals can be misled by well-meaning sellers who do not intend to cause problems; the motivation is more that of saving a few dollars.

A search of the county public deed records would have shown that there were two owners of the property George thought he had bought. Both owners needed to sign the deed that granted the property to George. Had George insisted that he receive title insurance when he bought, a local title insurance company would have done a search and made certain that George received good

119

title to the property through a properly drafted and recorded deed. George thought he was saving money. Instead, it took more than a year, and some expensive legal actions, to clear the title to the property. As it was, George was lucky, because he did eventually secure title.

Title insurance is just that: an insurance policy that guarantees that the condition of title to real property is as the title company reports it to be. It should be understood that title insurance does not guarantee that the title is good or perfect; the policy merely insures that title condition is as the title report indicates.

Title to real property is conveyed by documents called *deeds*. Deeds are further divided into special types that convey title in various ways, something your attorney will be familiar with. In most if not all counties or boroughs in this nation, deeds are recorded in the courthouse or hall of records. Recording means that permanent or archival copies of deeds are made, and these copies are kept permanently, available to the public in order that everyone may be informed as to who owns what. The owner of a property can be determined by checking who received title in the most recently recorded deed. All instruments that affect the title, such as liens, mortgages, trust deeds, or contracts, are recorded in the same manner as deeds, as are rights-of-way and any other burdens or agreements that affect the real property.

Title companies provide the service of searching the records in order to uncover all recorded documents (instruments) that affect a parcel of real property. Typically, after the title search, title companies issue a preliminary title report, which is their written compilation of the condition of the title. This preliminary report constitutes an offer to issue insurance in a given amount (usually the amount of the proposed purchase) that will insure a purchaser that the condition of the title is as stated in the report.

Judging title adequacy is complicated and should not be attempted by the inexperienced. An attorney in the state where the property is located, and having experience in real estate matters, is best qualified to interpret title matters.

Not all rights that affect real property are revealed by title searches. Title insurance policies use standard exclusions in order not to be liable for rights of others that are not recorded and are therefore not on their title report. Special kinds of title policies may be available in the area, insuring against some defects not revealed by recorded documents.

An example of such a title problem would be a roadway across the property you are interested in, when that roadway has been used for many years as access to another property located behind your subject property. When such a roadway is not allowed by a specific grant of right-of-way or easement, it would not be specifically set forth in a title report because no recorded documents mention it. Nevertheless, if such a road has been used for a good number of years as access to the other property, that property owner may have gained certain legal rights to use the road, even though it may cross your land. Such "easements of use" or "prescriptive easements" are fairly common in rural areas.

Some special title policies involve a survey of the insured land by a registered surveyor. Such surveys may discover defects such as buildings that are built over boundary lines, roadways that are not located accurately on their rights-of-way, or other such discrepancies. These defects are insured against when a policy covering them is purchased.

Boundaries, or property lines, are sometimes points of disagreement between rural property owners. This may stem from the fact that on larger tracts of rural land, especially in regions of the nation that are comparatively new to population and development, little actual surveying may have been done. Sometimes in the West, only the original government survey, done in the middle to late 1800s, and then sometimes with questionable accuracy, is available from which to determine boundaries. Old-time owners built fences from section or land claim corners, and these fences often followed the path of least resistance rather than being exactly straight or on the property line.

This past freedom in fence location may result in a problem later when an accurate survey determines the property line to be a few or even hundreds of feet away. Many such cases have been to court for settlement, with decisions sometimes favoring the fence and sometimes the survey. The larger the rural acreage and the more remote the location, the greater the chance for property lines and corners that may be obscure or inaccurately indicated. Practice in different states may vary in resolving such problems, but good advice in all areas is to avoid boundary conflicts. Surveys are one method of doing so, although in some cases a survey may be prohibitively expensive.

Land surveys are done only by registered surveyors, with most states requiring certification. High standards of accuracy and ethics are necessary in the surveying profession. Experience in any given geographic area is helpful, because the surveyor must know where established survey markers or points are in order to survey new lands. While recorded surveys locate such points for all to see and find, most surveyors, while working in a location, will establish their own control points from which to do future work. There is no requirement to record such markers. Accordingly, knowing which surveyor has been working in an area can be a key in procuring additional survey work in the area by the same surveyor at reasonable cost.

When the U.S. government surveyed much of the West during the mid to late 1800s, land was laid out in townships six miles square. Each square mile, or section, was then established by marking the section corners within the township. Though many of the old surveys were remarkably accurate, some were not. In the worst scenarios, government surveyors marked corners more or less haphazardly or not at all, writing their survey notes from hotel rooms or the local saloon.

Where marked on the ground, accurate or not, old government section corners are the basis for modern surveys. Done in a day when mechanical measurement with chains (measuring devices that were made up of many links and resembled chains) was the only way to determine distance, and angles were turned with optical transits, these corners are not as accurate as points set by modern methods. But for the very good reason that all subsequent surveys, and consequently all property boundaries, began with those original points, they cannot readily be corrected. You can imagine the horror if every property line in town had to be shifted six feet to the east.

Modern survey methods utilize instruments that receive signals from three satellites to precisely pinpoint a spot on the ground. Point-to-point distance on the ground is determined mathematically from two satellite shots, or—if one point can be seen from another—an electronic instrument measures the time required for a signal to cross the intervening distance. These highly accurate instruments speed survey work and result in economies.

Once a property is surveyed, a legal description can be written. This description is merely a recital of the boundaries of the property in terms of distance and bearing (direction). An overly simplified legal description might read: "From a iron pin, 200 feet north; thence 200 feet east; thence 200 feet south; thence 200 feet west to the point of beginning." Actually, it is necessary to locate this hypothetical 200-foot square in relation to other property, so the description would read "Beginning at the northwest corner of section 10, thence 150 feet east to an iron pin, the true point of beginning . . ." Thus the legal description developed from the survey not only describes the property boundaries accurately, but locates the property in relation to adjoining properties. Legal descriptions form the basis for the work of title companies. Descriptions are checked to make sure that there is no overlap onto adjoining properties. Obviously, if the legal description of property A, when staked out on the ground, overlaps 10 feet onto property B, B's owner is going to be unhappy. Then the question arises as to which survey is correct. Because most title companies and surveyors work competently in this area, few present-day errors go undetected. In those cases where errors do surface, if title insurance was purchased by the damaged party, that party might be reimbursed up to the amount of the insurance.

In some areas of the nation, real property titles had been registered by the Torrens system until lately. Here an actual history of the title chain (succession of owners) is kept in a book called an abstract of title. One result of this system is that few individuals except attorneys experienced in real estate practices are qualified to judge the condition of a title. Abstracts of title have nearly disappeared from most states, even in remote areas where few land sales occur. It is still possible to encounter this antiquated system, which may make title insurance unavailable or very expensive on certain properties. Take heed here, and if conventional title insurance, from recognized underwriters, cannot be issued by title companies, you *do* need the services of an attorney to interpret the condition of the title of country real estate you purchase.

Title insurance underwriters are regulated by each state, usually under the state government's insurance commissioner. Title and escrow companies are normally regulated by a state real estate division, presided over by a real estate commissioner.

14

Escrows

Among real estate brokers and salespeople, there is a tendency to use terminology in talking with prospective buyers and sellers that is not familiar to these customers and clients. The professional terminology and jargon that these licensees use among themselves is also used when brokers or salespeople talk with their contacts. Embarrassment often prevents customers and clients from asking for clarification when these terms are not understood, and a degree of uncertainty results. Unfortunately, the terms so used are sometimes not accurate or serve as a screen when the licensee is uncertain about details. If you hear a term with which you are not familiar, by all means ask for a definition. An effort has been made in this book to avoid such terms when possible and to describe ideas and situations in plain language.

The term *escrow* refers to the holding of a written agreement by a neutral third party until some conditions or actions are completed. In real estate transactions, the written agreement is usually the purchase contract between buyer and seller. The conditions or actions to be completed may be a survey or issuance of permits, but in most cases it will be the payment of money and signing of documents called for in the agreement.

Escrows generally may be handled by title companies, attorneys, real estate brokers in some states, escrow companies, banks, and institutions. In most states, those handling real estate escrows are licensed directly or indirectly and are regulated by the state.

The details to be completed in an escrow are written in a list known as the escrow instructions. The escrow officer sees to it

125

that the instructions of both buyer and seller are followed and that all details are completed. In most real estate transactions, those details may include the following:

- Preparing title transfer documents
- Receiving money from buyer
- Paying agreed-upon costs or bills
- Paying liens and recording evidence of payment
- Prorating or dividing property taxes based upon time
- Preparing loan documents
- Issuing title insurance
- Paying proceeds to seller
- Recording deed to new owner
- Federal tax reporting

Most title companies today are more or less full-service institutions. Escrow officers are highly skilled and perform many additional functions that crop up in real estate sales. Government-mandated forms of many sorts, including the reams of paperwork associated with any government guaranteed loan program, as well as sales proceeds reporting for income tax purposes, are routinely processed in escrow. Such procedural loads are out of the question for most of us, and yet escrow officers perform these tasks daily.

It is not unusual for questions to arise during closing, usually because some tiny detail has not been foreseen. Escrow officers must maintain a strict neutrality, and yet their approach to these challenges can go a long way toward reaching a rapid and amiable agreement between buyer and seller. Because they handle the settlement (closing) of several sales daily, their experience rapidly becomes broader than that of the average real estate broker or attorney.

Don't expect an escrow officer to offer opinions or advice on a transaction. Strict neutrality must be observed in order to maintain the neutrality of the escrow. An officer may be able to discuss general practices within the scope of the escrow duties, but generally there is a very real reluctance to discuss matters that may be categorized as legal advice.

Escrows may be established for special purposes. One such is the *collection escrow,* which can be established to accept regular payments when the buyer makes payments directly to the seller, as in owner financing. Such an escrow provides many safeguards. Payments made voluntarily by the purchaser are accepted by the escrow and are applied to interest and principal as agreed upon in the instructions. If the payments are late or not made at all, the escrow company has no obligation to collect, despite the name collection escrow. Curing default is still the responsibility of the seller.

Though basically a bookkeeping service, collection escrows have benefits for both buyer and seller. Many owners who provide financing are capable of doing the bookkeeping involved in receiving payments; however, it is best to leave the calculations of interest and principal to a neutral third party. Most escrow companies and banks use computers to calculate interest and maintain records. Monthly or annual statements are provided for buyer and seller.

Perhaps the most valuable use of collection escrows is to hold those documents that must be recorded when the obligation is paid in order to remove the lien from the record. If payments are made directly to the seller providing owner financing, those documents are often not in existence during the time the payments are being made. Such documents as reconveyances, and satisfactions of mortgage or deeds when contracts are used, are common and necessary instruments in purchase and financing transactions. Much difficulty can be avoided by having a reconveyance, satisfaction of mortgage, or deed prepared initially and held in the collection escrow for delivery to the buyer when the obligation is fully paid. Doing so may avoid searching for the seller at the time the obligation is paid. The seller may be unavailable, deceased, or now unwilling to execute evidence to be recorded stating that the obligation is paid. In such instances, having held such instruments in the collection escrow would be a boon. Expensive and time-consuming court actions will be avoided.

Holding reconveyances, satisfactions, and deeds in the collection escrow is safe for the seller, because the escrow cannot deliver such instruments to the buyer until the obligation is satisfied. The escrow company will know when that occurs, because they are collecting the payments and doing the record keeping. Such instruments cannot be trusted to the purchaser before that time, because once recorded, they effectively remove evidence of the obligation as far as the record is concerned.

In many country areas, when a property is purchased from and financed by the owner, the entire transaction is set forth on a *contract* or *contract for deed.* In such cases, actual title to the property is not given to the purchaser at that time. Title will pass at a later time, usually when the financial obligations have been satisfied. The deed, passing title to the new owner, should be prepared initially and placed into the collection escrow with appropriate instructions. Both parties are protected: The buyer will not receive the deed unless the property is paid for, and the buyer knows the deed is there and will be delivered when the property is paid for.

The neutrality of a collection escrow protects both buyer and seller. Escrows do not favor the interests of one party over another; instead, they explicitly follow instructions. Flexibility is another benefit to the parties, for collection escrow instructions can allow for any number of variables or for changing the nature of a security document at a certain point. An example would be the conversion of a purchase contract to a mortgage, the benefits of which can be explained by your attorney. Another function might be to prepare and record documents granting clear title to a portion of the property after the balance owing is reduced to a certain point. In short, a collection escrow can function hand in hand with the many possibilities owner financing allows, providing the protection of strict compliance to both parties.

Title companies provide other services as well. Many will contract with private lenders, such as sellers who are carrying the financing on property they sold, to search the record and determine whether obligations in the financing agreement are being fulfilled, such as the timely payment of real property taxes. Generally speaking, title companies are able to search only public records. In other words, the data they convey are all part of public records, which are available to you and me at the courthouse or hall of records. Their advantage is expertise at searching out and compiling the recorded data.

15

Finding and Buying Your Country Property

Your homework on the geographic area has been completed and you are certain of the region in which you want to live. You have even determined that the kind of spot you dream about *does* exist in the area. You are aware of some of the small compromises that will be necessary in order for your dream place to become reality, and you are willing to compromise on minor physical details. Such adjustments in your thinking will greatly help you understand the area and the way of life there. Now, what is the best way to go about finding a specific spot in that area? Country properties that are for sale are found in many different ways.

Sellers of real estate fall into two general categories. The first category includes sellers with a medium to high motivation to sell, who are making an effort to do so. Included here are sellers who *must* sell, such as a seller who has been transferred and is moving to another area at a certain time, and estates, where the property must be sold to satisfy debts of the estate. In these instances, the motivation to sell is strong, so that at the very least, some action to bring about a sale is being taken. This may involve hiring an agent to sell the property, running ads in the newspaper, or similar steps. A seller who owns an acreage parcel and wants, but is not compelled, to sell would also be a motivated seller.

The second category of sellers includes those who are not highly motivated but would sell if they could secure the "right" price. There may or may not be active steps being taken toward procuring a sale. Sellers in this group make up a sizable portion of total sellers at any one time and probably constitute the majority of sellers of bare acreage.

So how do you find sellers of country real estate? One way is to look in the "For Sale" ads in the real estate section of the local newspapers of the region you want to live in. Depending on the size of the newspaper and the area, the real estate section may be further classified into two or more sections, one for homes and one for acreages. Such ads commonly have a short description of the property and the price. A phone call to the seller will uncover more details.

If you are looking beforehand—that is, before your need is compelling—you can subscribe to the local paper from the area in which you are interested. Reading the "For Sale by Owner" ads will keep you up-to-date as new properties come on the market. Being familiar with the area will be very helpful in understanding location when you talk with sellers of properties that interest you. This type of search can be carried on even if you live a great distance from the area.

If your search is a very active one and you are in the area where you wish to locate, you can drive all of the country roads in the area that most appeals to you. It is nearly impossible to spend much time driving out in the country without coming across property that is for sale. Sometimes there will be only a phone number for you to follow up on. With country homes, you may be able to inquire within.

Another good way to find out what is for sale in a country area is to inquire at local activity hubs, such as country stores and gas stations. Often there is common knowledge about what is for sale among the local people. Don't expect accurate information about any specific property when that information is second-hand. Find out the location of the property and the identity of the seller, then contact the seller for details.

If you wish to carry on a full-scale search for property within an area you have identified as ideal, you need some way of contacting most or all of the owners in that area. By doing that, you will discover what properties are presently on the market, as well as those that the owner may sell if asked to do so. To accomplish this kind of canvass, you would need to go door to door over the entire area. If it is sparsely populated countryside, most of the area can be covered within a reasonable time, except that not everyone is at home during the day. Neighbors can give you much data about who lives next door and possibly provide phone numbers so that you can call in the evening. If you decide to embark on this kind of a search, by its completion you will know the area far better than those who live there!

Of course, you can't talk to a piece of unimproved land. Even the neighbor may not know who owns an adjoining acreage. But there is a way that you can contact owners of unimproved land. In each county's assessor's office, usually located in the courthouse in the county seat, are records of every parcel of real property located in that county. These are public records that give the acreage, owner, owner's address, assessed value, most recent taxes, and a wealth of additional data. Such things as zoning, whether or not the property is improved with a dwelling, even construction and assessment data on the dwelling and other buildings may be included. All you need to do is correlate the properties on the map with their actual locations out in the country. Sometimes aerial photographs of large areas are available to help you with this.

The easiest and most common way to find a parcel of country real estate is to inquire at a local real estate office. Before you do this, there are a number of things you should know that will allow you to benefit most from the services real estate brokerages offer.

First and most important is the fact that the real estate agent will not be representing you. Unless you have specifically agreed to hire, and pay, a real estate agent, that agent is working for the seller. Remember this when, after much contact with the agent, you find yourself thinking and talking about "my" agent. He or she isn't "your" agent unless you have hired that person in writing. The differences in the agent representing one party or the other may be slight or great, depending on the circumstances. Real estate departments in all states strive for high standards within the industry, and civil law more or less enforces many of those standards. There are still caveats, however, when an agent is representing the other party in a two-party transaction.

One factor to consider is that even though an agent is required to disclose to you, the buyer, all pertinent facts *about* the property, there may be other details not directly pertaining to the physical property itself that could be left unsaid to bring about a sale.

Remember that an agent has a moral and legal responsibility to secure the most beneficial price for his client, the seller. Even so, most real estate agents with good reputations do an excellent job of balancing the responsibilities to two parties in the same transaction. You can, of course, secure the services of an attorney, or possibly another real estate broker, either of whom you must compensate, to advise you if you do not feel secure in your own judgment.

When contacting a real estate agent to help you in your search for country property, it is important to locate the agency that is most active out in country areas. Not only will that office have the largest selection of properties for sale in the country area among their own listings, but more important, they will have agents who are knowledgeable about country property. This will avoid the wasted time, and possible misunderstandings that can arise, when a city- or town-oriented salesperson tries to work on a rural property.

Many times in a small town and surrounding rural area, there will be half a dozen local real estate brokers. One or two of these will probably specialize on properties located in rural areas. The experience of an agent who constantly works with country properties can be invaluable to you in your search.

Avoid the mistake of mixing looking on your own and working with a broker. And even more important, avoid entering into negotiations directly with any seller who has the property listed for sale with a broker. Doing so can place the seller in jeopardy of breaking his listing contract, with legal consequences.

If you decide you are capable of finding suitable property on your own and negotiating the purchase on your own, this is a good way to proceed provided you are experienced enough to do so. This method may or may not save you money. You will probably discover some properties that are not listed for sale with local agencies. If you exhaust the possibilities on your own, you can then go to a broker. Once you contact an agent and that agent begins showing you property, you will likely be exposed to all of the offerings that are listed in the area.

BEFORE YOU BUY

Here is a checklist of some of the more important points that should be clear in your mind, and evaluated, before you buy:

- Unimproved land
  1. Boundaries and corners
  2. Access
  3. Zoning and restrictions (May you build a home there?)
  4. Approval for septic
  5. Water prospects
  6. Availability of utilities
  7. Presence of easements
  8. Drainage (Is there any wet-weather ponding or flows? Wetlands?)
- Acreage with a home
  1. Boundaries and corners
  2. Access
  3. Zoning and restrictions (May you add onto the home?)
  4. Presence of easements
  5. Drainage
  6. Condition of structures
  7. Condition and adequacy of water supply
  8. Condition and adequacy of sewage disposal system

An important step before finalizing a purchase of property that includes an existing home is to have the home inspected. Few of us are fully qualified to judge the condition of structures. In nearly every area, qualified home inspection services are available. It is to your benefit to know the condition of a property you are considering. A full report would include inspecting and reporting on all elements of the structure. Items that were not according to code or were in less than good condition, including electrical and plumbing, would be noted. An inspection would be made for dry rot and wood-eating insects. Foundation condition, moisture, and storm drainage might be included. All of this is valuable information to a prospective buyer. Since an inspection establishes a professional opinion of the condition of the property at the time of sale, it can also benefit the seller, because full disclosure is accomplished. It is common for inspections to be a part of the original offer to purchase, with the purchaser retaining the right to cancel if the inspection reveals conditions that are other than those represented.

It is not unusual for there to be defects in a home of which the seller is not aware. If the inspection reveals such a defect, it is often possible to negotiate with the seller to have repairs done and split the cost. An agent might explain to the seller that the defect exists and should be repaired, and the purchaser would benefit because that particular item is now assured of being in good condition.

BUYING THE PROPERTY

Look at enough property to be able to judge value in the area where you are interested. After looking at only one place, you will not know if the price being asked is fair or not because you are unfamiliar with values in the area. But look at a few more places, and soon a relationship between features and price becomes clear. What happens is that you unconsciously use the comparison method of determining value, the same method that professionals working in real estate use. If a property with certain features is priced lower than similar properties in the area with the same features, by comparison you make the judgment that the property is a good value.

It is important to have enough exposure to real property in an area to make value judgments, whether you look on your own or use the services of an agency. Given a choice of properties with appropriate features, the property that delivers the desired features and is the best buy is the one most often chosen. This is not to imply that an unlimited number of properties with the qualities you seek will be available in the country. Most likely there will be only a few or, possibly, in some areas, only one.

ON YOUR OWN

If you find your dream property while searching on your own, the next step is negotiating the purchase with the seller. If both parties are knowledgeable and in agreement, it may be possible to structure the transaction to the maximum benefit of both buyer and seller. Chapter 12 discusses some of the benefits and flexibilities of seller financing. Probably the most important aspect at this point is to determine the details of the sale and to get those details down in writing on a purchase agreement that both parties sign, and that becomes a legally binding contract.

This is an excellent time for you to decide whether you will need the services of an attorney in the transaction. If so, your attorney can prepare a simple purchase agreement, accept a deposit as earnest money, and handle the closing of the sale. A title company will likely be used to provide a preliminary title report and to issue title insurance at closing. Some attorneys may prefer to use the services of the local title or escrow company to close the sale. *Closing* means the payment of final moneys due under the purchase agreement and the signing and recording of all documents.

Knowledgeable buyers and sellers can prepare their own purchase agreements, likely using the same standard forms used by local real estate companies. These forms, and others prepared by certain legal publishers, are commonly available at stationery or office-supply stores. If the parties complete their own purchase agreement, the earnest money or deposit should be placed in the title company that will close the sale and issue title insurance.

Although different regions approach division of closing costs in various ways, some items are more or less standard as to which party pays. In many areas, the title insurance premium is paid by the seller, who usually agrees to provide clear, insured title. Escrow fees, the fees charged for handling all of the details, document preparation, and closing, are split equally between parties, because both benefit. Document-recording fees are often paid by the party benefiting from the document. Real estate taxes are usually prorated as of the date of possession of the property. Taxes due before that time are an obligation of the seller, and taxes after that time are paid by the buyer. Satisfying liens on the property is, unless otherwise agreed upon, the obligation of the seller.

In most instances when an attorney is involved, the attorney fees will be paid by the party who is being represented by that attorney.

It is possible to negotiate different division of costs if good reason exists to do so or both parties are willing. Certain fees, however, such as costs related to some federally insured loan programs, are apportioned to the seller or buyer by statute and cannot be changed. Various lending institutions have rules relating to some costs. In the case of seller financing, fortunately, common sense and the will of the parties to accomplish mutual benefits can prevail.

Length of time in escrow—the time between signing the purchase agreement and the closing of the sale—varies, basically to allow time for certain acts. The seller may need to find and purchase another property, or the buyer may have funds coming at a certain time in the future. Such considerations form the basis for establishing the date of escrow closing. In the absence of compelling reasons on the part of either party, a thirty- or forty-five-day escrow would not be unreasonable. During that time, the title company will complete a preliminary title report, gather information and figures, and prepare the documents to close the escrow on the agreed date.

Purchasing through an Agency

One advantage of purchasing through an agency is that if you make an offer that is below the asking price, the agent is the one who presents that offer to the seller. Such direct negotiation is sometimes viewed as confrontational and is difficult for many people when they are involved as one of the parties. Here, a skilled agent is often able to make valuable contributions. These include guiding you, the purchaser, in structuring an offer so that it has the highest chance of acceptance, as well as presenting sound reasons to a seller why a particular offer might be in the best interest of that seller. Sometimes an experienced agent can soothe a seller who is offended by an offer that is deemed too low. If that same offer were presented by you, the buyer, directly, a serious deterioration in negotiations might occur.

It is not unusual to find that an offer presented through the seller's agent is accepted, even though that offer was well below the asking price. That is because the agent is knowledgeable and able to demonstrate to the seller that the offer does equate with the true value of the property, or that timeliness of the sale is more important than the highest price, or that the sale at this time on these terms meets other needs of the seller that the agent is aware of, but that you probably don't know about.

Another advantage of procuring the services of a real estate agency is that the agency will make sure that the various steps leading to, and including, the closing take place. The agent will be familiar with the way closing costs are normally divided in that area. Sometimes this means help with securing the necessary loans. The only things you, the purchaser, have to do is make sure that you are able to complete your portion of the bargain, which is usually to have the balance of the down payment and costs available at the closing.

Some title companies make copies of the preliminary title report available to the purchaser prior to closing. Doing so makes sense, in the event that there are title conditions you feel need additional explanation. If you have procured an attorney to advise you in the purchase details, your attorney will secure the preliminary report and examine it. If any communication with the seller is necessary, the attorney will probably contact the agent through whom you purchased.

On the closing date, the title company will witness and notarize signatures of both buyer and seller on the various documents involved and receive the necessary funds to complete payment under the terms of the purchase agreement. At the closing, escrow officers are able to explain routine documents and procedures but are unable to offer any other advice, such as legal advice. This is because the escrow officer must remain a neutral third party to the transaction.

As a purchaser, you might wish to consider one of the many home buyer insurance plans available. These policies differ from fire insurance in that they insure the condition of and repairs to the home and would cover the costs of such things as water heaters, furnaces, or structural elements of the home should repair or replacement become necessary during the warranty period. Normally this period would be one year, the usual time required for a new owner to uncover all the "bugs" in a property. Most agents have access to a variety of such plans.

---◆---

16

The Country Frame of Mind

Elbert and his wife were in their mid-fifties when they purchased a small acreage beside the highway a few miles from a small Oregon town and retired to the country. Elbert had been in business in Los Angeles and had lots of energy to spend building their retirement home. He proceeded to build a house exactly in the middle of their acreage. It was a large house, with all of the amenities and conveniences. It became noticeable as construction progressed that this was a house designed for the city. The modernistic architectural style looked out of place in the pastoral setting. Painted exterior walls and trim, with no attempt to blend into the site, contributed to the incompatibility of the structure with the land.

Next Elbert fenced his entire acreage with a high, woven-wire fence on pipe posts. As the land was on a slight slope upward from the highway, all of the land, including the fence, was visible to everyone passing. Soon large masonry gateposts appeared, with a huge wrought-iron gate hung between, blocking unauthorized access (and his neighbors' access as well.) Oversize, gaudy light fixtures were installed atop the posts, and at night two distractingly bright orbs of light blasted out at the neighbors and all who passed by.

Elbert then ran out of things to do, so making use of a new riding mower, he methodically mowed every inch of those few acres on a regular basis. Neighbors passing by would smile in amusement at Elbert's attempt to create a city lot environment.

Soon Elbert purchased a business in the nearby town, which put him in contact with most of the small-business people in the area. Elbert's business experience was gained in a huge city, where if one or a few customers were offended, there were always plenty more. That had become his philosophy. But the small-town business community consisted of only a few dozen key people, and when Elbert's blunt, offensive ways caused them to stop dealing with him, business slowed.

Elbert couldn't figure out what was happening and decided he needed to become more visible in the community. He began attending town council and school board meetings, where he was generous with his views of how things should be and how they had been where he came from. He frequently explained how various practices of running the town, and its schools, were much inferior to what he was accustomed to.

Instead of accepting elements of the small-town ways, Elbert tried to change them. He continually compared the area to the city environment he had left. Not surprisingly, Elbert's business dropped still more, and within a few months he had sold it. He became very bitter, allowing his thinking to dwell on everything he felt was wrong in the community. Eventually, he asked me to sell his property, and he and his wife returned to the city.

While Elbert's case may be extreme, it does offer a good lesson to residents moving from the city to the country. Elbert wanted to move to the country, but he wanted to take the city with him, and he made no attempt to understand the ways of the country. Luckily, nearly everyone can make the transition to the different country lifestyle, if they give it a chance.

It is recognized that country living is at a more leisurely pace. But much more than a just "slowing down" is necessary before a new resident really fits in. Nearly every aspect of day-to-day living is different in some way than in a metropolitan area. When thought is given to these differences, good reasons for them are readily found. Those reasons usually are sound enough that the country is not going to change to accommodate an individual like Elbert. Rather, all of the Elberts who successfully adapt to a country lifestyle change at least some of their attitudes and expectations.

Employment often requires an adjustment, because what is available may differ greatly from what were accustomed city norms, in more ways than just compensation. Working for a large company in the city can be impersonal, involving little contact with those other than immediate supervisors and other workers. Contrast this with employment in rural areas, where often there is nearly constant contact with the owner, who also may be the only supervisor. There may be just a handful of other workers, and the employee may be in direct contact with the customers. In order to fit into the requirements of the job in this example, the employee must adjust to working closely with the boss, who will establish the way the job is to be done. At the same time, the employee will be interacting with customers who are also neighbors in a small-town environment. The job, the boss, and the customers preexisted in this equation and are unlikely to change in expectations or attitudes just because the employee thinks they should. The adjustment must be made by the employee.

This is not to say that better ways of doing things cannot be introduced. But introduction of change is more successful once the employee has been accepted by the boss and customers. This same familiarization time gives the newcomer a chance to evaluate former ideas and impressions from the perspective of the new country environment. With this new perspective, it may become evident that there are good reasons why the job should be performed just as it has been.

With time spent and experience gained in the country, new residents quickly discover that personal reputation is very important in rural and small-town life. In city environments, the people with whom we come into contact fade mysteriously away outside of the familiar context where we are accustomed to seeing them. Your doctor, dentist, grocer, neighbor, and boss all fulfill their roles, but normally we do not see them other than in those roles. In the small town, however, you may see each of these people every day, and in other than their professional or business establishments. Most aspects of your daily life are known to your small-town neighbors, and you know theirs. Something about this relationship often brings out the best in people, not a small reason why living in the country is enjoyable.

Take big-city expectations on country shopping excursions, and you are going to be in trouble. With major franchises and large chain stores locating in smaller and smaller towns, shopping in the rural areas of America offers much wider choices than in years past. But many specialty stores city dwellers may be accustomed to will not be present. Selection of most goods, even within chain stores, will be poorer. Many new country residents are surprised at how many times they hear, "We can order it for you." Allowing this restriction in availability to become a sore point will be very damaging to the adaptation of a new resident and will help create a bad attitude. Certain advantages have certain trade-offs; here, the slower pace of living that small populations enjoy offsets the poorer selection of goods available.

Specialty services also are fewer. There may be only one or two restaurants in town. Two doctors and one dentist, along with several nurses, may make up the local medical center. Again, it is unrealistic to expect the same level of services that were available in the city. Remember that it takes the massed population of a metropolitan area to support the services that exist there. To expect the same level of services in the lightly populated country is to hold to unreasonable expectations.

Country schools often far surpass city institutions as far as quality of education is concerned. True, very small schools are not always able to offer the wide-ranging curriculum that a large, well-funded city school may provide. But other advantages offset this. There is often a more favorable teacher-to-student ratio, and teachers are often more creative and effective in their jobs.

Few school districts are free of budgetary problems today, whether in the country or city. Generally, the country teacher has more latitude to solve problems brought on by funding shortfalls. In small systems, there is more contact between teachers and parents, and between parents and the school district. Bureaucracies are much smaller and hold officials more accountable. Activities of the local school board are reported in the local media and are widely read about, leading to better participation.

The total results are schools in small-town and rural areas that have excellent records. In many country areas, the percentage of students who attend college is higher than for city schools. SAT scores are often higher, not necessarily because country and small-town students are smarter, but because parents, teachers, and neighbors are more closely involved in the lives of the students, and the students often respond to this interest and concern by better applying themselves while in school. Thus the learning environment is encouraged.

Another aspect of country and small-town school life is athletics. An important formative element in schools no matter where they are located, sports perhaps generate greater enthusiasm in rural and small-town areas. Many rural schools today, facing severe budget crunches, find their athletic programs either completely or partially funded by students, their parents, alumni, and other interested parties. This is done in addition to normal school district taxes.

It would be inaccurate to state that rural and small-town schools do not have drug problems. In actuality, this scourge is almost universal throughout America. The advantages of smaller towns and rural areas is that organized drug distribution is not as likely. While availability is a fact and may pose a constant temptation even in the small town, the organized gang and peer pressure may not yet exist to the same extent as in cities.

If you move to the country hoping to keep children in the dark ages, however, disappointment awaits. Alternative dress styles and personal adornment practices are present in small-town environments too. The media, particularly television, are full of models for young people about how the "cool" should dress, act, live, and perhaps most puzzling of all, what their attitude should be. That attitude is not always good. What is encouraging is that in small-town areas, friends and neighbors not only take active interests in youth, but also are in closer contact with them for more of the time. There are many positive things for young people to do, and there is less violence. Negative examples spread by the media have less effect on young people when many positive adult examples to the contrary are evident.

If you are to enjoy living in a semi-isolated region where residents are not numerous and towns are small, be prepared to accept road systems where important roads may not be as wide or well surfaced as you are accustomed to.

The roads in rural areas are funded in various ways, but counties with light populations and small tax bases have a harder time generating revenue for maintaining existing road systems, let alone improvement or new construction. If a particular chuckhole is bothering you, perhaps the best thing to do is offer to fill it yourself. After all, you moved to the area because it had the advantages of few people. Realize ahead of time that this small population, though an advantage in quality of life and slow pace, also means that resources are limited, and residents may need to get individually involved or form groups to do such things as fix the chuckholes.

Cultural events are lacking in many rural areas. This does not mean, however, that rural area residents are all culturally deficient. What it does mean is that sufficient audience or participation is unavailable in the region to support such events or institutions. The cure is to travel to areas where the desired opportunities are available.

Some also may view country regions as being lacking in recreational opportunities. If recreation means going to big-league ball games, this may be true. If it means outdoor recreation, however, then opportunities are far more numerous than in city areas. City residents can spend many hours just driving to a recreational site. When you live in the country, these sites may be very close by.

As soon as small towns begin to grow, costs go up, not always delivering more or better services in the process. Costs increase for law enforcement, a bigger fire department, planners, building officials, a town court system, a larger sewage plant, and perhaps a new waterworks. Growth incurs these costs, some of which may be new. If large numbers of new residents from the city move to an area, there will be expectations for the town to provide more and more services for the residents. Established traditions may fall by the wayside, either because of lack of discipline or because that tradition is unwieldy now in face of the greater population. In some former small towns that have grown, the tradition of townspeople painting city hall every five years no longer draws enthusiasm or participation.

No, a small-town softball team is not world class. The fire engine is not the latest model. But the ball team has a lot of fun, and it helps residents get to know one another only as sports participation can. And the fire engine has adequate capacity; it just doesn't have all the bells and whistles of machines five years newer. The fact that these elements may not measure up completely to standards of their city counterparts is irrelevant. They are exactly right for where they are. Many small towns will upgrade their fire equipment to the most modern available and train their firemen to operate in the most advanced manner. Doing so may strain their budget and directly increase taxes, but if the townspeople decide together to do these things, the effort will not only be successful, but will meld the community closer together as well. After all, the residents all struggled together for years to make do with what they had.

Living in the country will be most enjoyable for those who are lucky enough to set aside any expectations formed by years of living in cities enjoying services and benefits that can exist only where large numbers of people create viable markets. These viable markets also become viable hotbeds for all sorts of maladies that form the main reason why the city became intolerable. It is unreasonable to expect the same level of services when you specifically do not expect the same level of problems.

An attitude of tolerance and an awareness of compromise will do a great deal to speed adjustment to country living. Acceptance of the status quo, at least until you understand the reason for it, will endear you to your fellow residents. When indications that change is appropriate do surface, let that change be in the direction of making things better in that country area, rather than trying to make the country area more like the city.

Remember your initial reasons for desiring to move to the country. Once you become a country dweller, do not forget what it was that motivated you to come home to the country. Learn about the ecology; be aware of the environment. In so doing, your enjoyment of the new country life will be enhanced. Give thought to your stewardship of your little part of the country. This will ensure that the same things that drew you here will remain for your children, and your children's children.